SIGNS OF THE END TIMES

SIGNS OF THE END TIMES

RACHEL TEJEDA MORRIS

Signs of the End Times by Rachel Tejeda Morris

This book is written to provide information and motivation to readers. Its purpose is not to render any type of psychological, legal, or professional advice of any kind. The content is the sole opinion and expression of the author, and not necessarily that of the publisher.

Copyright © 2021 by Rachel Tejeda Morris

All rights reserved. No part of this book may be reproduced, transmitted, or distributed in any form by any means, including, but not limited to, recording, photocopying, or taking screenshots of parts of the book, without prior written permission from the author or the publisher. Brief quotations for noncommercial purposes, such as book reviews, permitted by Fair Use of the U.S. Copyright Law, are allowed without written permissions, as long as such quotations do not cause damage to the book's commercial value. For permissions, write to the publisher, whose address is stated below.

Printed in the United States of America.

ISBN 978-1-955363-06-8 (Paperback)
ISBN 978-1-955363-07-5 (Digital)

Lettra Press books may be ordered through booksellers or by contacting:
Lettra Press LLC
30 N Gould St. Suite 4753
Sheridan, WY 828011
1 307-200-3414 | info@lettrapress.com
www.lettrapress.com

CONTENTS

Chapter 1   One By One 1
Chapter 2   Prophecies, To Be Fulfilled. 4
Chapter 3   As The World Continues 7
Chapter 4   Life Goes On 11
Chapter 5   We Need A Revival 13
Chapter 6   The World Is In A Chao's 15
Chapter 7   Quality Check 18
Chapter 8   Go With The Flow 21
Chapter 9   Getting Coronavirus 24
Chapter 10 One Day At A Time 28
Chapter 11 A Global Crisis 30
Chapter 12 A Wake Up Call 34
Chapter 13 A Great Awakening 39
Chapter 14 A Shield Of Protection 41
Chapter 15 Wait On The Lord 44
Chapter 16 A Slow Come Back 47
Chapter 17 Facing The Unknown 52
Chapter 18 A Riot And Looting 55
Chapter 19 Behind The Scenes 57
Chapter 20 There's A Brighter Tomorrow 59
Chapter 21 Never Ending Story 62
Chapter 22 Going In Circles 65
Chapter 23 Moving Forward 69
Chapter 24 Working The Front Lines 71
Chapter 25 How To Talk To Others About Covid Masks 74

Chapter 26 Long-Short Term Effects From Coronavirus 77
Chapter 27 Trump On His Way Out Of The White House 79
Chapter 28 A Riot At The Capitol 81
Chapter 29 Time to Clean Up and Clear Out 83
Chapter 30 What Does Twitter Have To Say 85
Chapter 31 To See The Perspective Of The Other Side 87
Chapter 32 A Taste Of The Iceberg 89
Chapter 33 Help In Need, Tracking The Virus 91
Chapter 34 A Texans Water Crisis 93
Chapter 35 The Texas Tribune 94
Chapter 36 Tracking The Virus 96
Chapter 37 Which Vaccine Is Right For You To Get 99
Chapter 38 A Year Living With Coronavirus 102
Chapter 39 A Time For Restoration 105
Chapter 40 It's Not Over Yet Be On Guard 107

CHAPTER ONE

ONE BY ONE

Living in an apartment building people die one by one. Living in a nursing home people die one by one. Living in an assisted living place, people die one by one. No matter where you go there is death and danger.

There is nowhere safe. They take guns to the schools and shoot the kids. They take guns to church and kill people. You're not safe in your own home. A little girl was doing her homework sitting at her dining room table. There happens to be a drive by shooting. So sad. The little girl was instantly killed.

There's no place safe. In assisted living, we are one small community. We are like family. I heard somebody yelling then I thought I was hearing things. I heard it again. I decided to find out who was making that noise. So I followed where the yelling was coming from. I got closer and closer and I asked, "Where are you?" They yelled, "I am down here." It was my neighbour, Aggie. She lived a few doors down from me. She was lying face down on the kitchen floor on her walker. She was also lying on her call alert button. So she could not call the staff for help. That is why she was yelling for help. Her door was opened, Thank God. I don't think I would have heard her yelling for help. She was bleeding a little from her glasses jabbing into her face as she hit the hardwood floor. I used my button to call for help and two men came and helped Aggie up. She just got back from the hospital. She did not want to go back there again. The man said "good job" to me. I just smiled and was glad I could have helped in any way that I could. Down in the dining room, Dorothy gasped for air. She begins to panic and shake and scream for help that she can not breath. Her oxygen tank is about empty. There is another woman whose name is Lyn, she gave Dorothy some oxygen. Dorothy began to calm down. Then everything went back to normal. Dorothy raised 8 children by herself, she is a widow. I should say her and the Lord because he is a husband to the widows. When she was younger, she owned a dress shop and she was an excellent sewer. You show her what you want and she would make it just like the picture that was shown to her. Dorothy was in hospice; she was dying slowly. One by one people began to disappear and one by one they died. The world is so corrupt now there's hardly any peace. Young men gamble to make money. Some get addicted to gambling so bad, they lose their home, their business, their family, everything. Same with the drug world. Whether you sell it, buy it, or use it. It is an addiction. Now there are a few men dressed up like women and do out call service. They also do stage drag, where they dress as a woman and lip sing to a CD. They make big money. They say this is the only way they know how to hustle money quickly. There are some people who give plasma to earn money. Between a couple they can make a good amount a month. I've seen guy's pretend they cannot walk and sit in a wheelchair begging for money. I've seen women stand in front of a store asking for money to get something to eat. Some collect cans and get money. Now the kids are not safe to play outside by themselves. They can be kidnapped and sold, or used for sex trafficing or human tafficing. The grown-ups are not safe either.

That's how dark and cold the world has gotten. Today people try to play God. They change their sex if they don't like what God made them when they were born. There are Christians being persecuted in other countries. And here we are complaining about our president. It's about the intentions of our hearts. Through the grace of Jesus Christ we are saved. We are seeing everything falling apart around the world. Just as the Bible says, "The time is near." We need to be fishers of men. Two blocks away from my apartment they had a shootout and a SWAT team.

Some man robbed the gas station. My girls were hanging out with their friends and they happened to see what was going on. What a sight for the kids to see. I don't think they were scared. They were fascinated more than anything. When they came home they told me what had happened. The kids were going to Taco Bell. The gas station was right across the street from Taco Bell. So the world is getting more corrupt by the day. Sickness gets worse. The weather gets out of control. Things happen just as the prophecies come to pass that were told in the Bible. There is more to come.

There's many in the old testament that were fulfilled already as well.

CHAPTER TWO

PROPHECIES, TO BE FULFILLED.

Prophecy or biblical prophecy comprises passages of the bible that reflect communications from God to humans. Through prophets to have seen revelations from God. Prophetic prophecy and signs, not politicians. For many evangelicals, Jerusalem is about prophecy not politics. Accurate predictions institute for creation research. Signs popular fulfilled Sept 8, 2019, the old testament filled with prophecies, signs, 2 kings 8:3

At the end of the seven years when the two men came back home they were told to restore everything to the woman that was lost to her. And the boy told the king that Elisha brought him back to life. The King wanted them to tell him some stories. He said to the men, "Is this true?" Then the men did as the King said. 1 chronicles 17:1 David has settled into his house.

When David was settled in a palace, he summoned Nathan the prophet. Look David said I am living in a beautiful cedar palace, but the ark of the Lord's covenant is out there in a tent. Nathan replied to David, "Do whatever you have in mind, for God is with you." But that same night God said to Nathan, "Go and tell my servant David this is what the Lord has declared, you are not the one to build a house for me to live in. I have never lived in a house from the day I brought the Israelites out of Egypt until this very day. My home has always been a tent, moving from one place to another a tabernacle. Yet no matter where I have gone with the Israelites, I have never once complained to Israel's leaders. The shepherds of my people. I have never asked them,

"Why haven't you built me a beautiful cedar house?" April 26 2012, the God of the Bible has many ways in which he makes himself known. Thousands of prophecies that prove the Bible have been fulfilled.

Passages, inspirations, interpretations, we can look back on history and see how the prophets proclaimed and predicted came to pass. They did not see it come to pass because they died. The prophet Daniel prophesied, the first and second coming of Christ. 400 years in bongage. The fall of the ten tribes of Israel Gen 15:13 God told Abraham his seed would be captives for 400 years in a strange land, but that God would judge that nation and bring them out. In Isaiah 7:8 Deut. 28

They will flee before their enemies if they fail to keep his commandments. Desolation and captivity of Judah prophesied. The 70 year rule of Babylon prophesied. Jer 25:11 God's personal visit at Belshazzar's party Dan. 9 :2 Isaiah 13:17 mentions Babylon also mentions that the Medes would do it. Daniel prophesied 3 more empires would fall. Daniel 11 Daniel went on to foretell even to the exact date when the Messiah would come and their temple as well as the city of Jerusalem shall be destroyed. The 70 weeks of Daniel's interpretation as preached by Rev. William Branham reveals the calculation to the 69 weeks to the exact date of 30 A.D. The exact time Jesus began to preach. Daniel prophesied 3 more empires rising after Babylon. Medo-Persia, Greece, and Rome came out just as he said. Daniel was so accurate as a prophet about the Greek wars that the opponents accused the writer of the book of backdating the word of God. They simply could not believe that someone could be so accurate. So they had to make a plan. They said that Daniel lived in the second century B.C. and wrote about Babylon.

However, close inspection will show you that he had more knowledge than most historians and archeologists who knew nothing of Belshazzar outside the book of Daniel. How could a fake not know what was not known to Historians? This story has captivated audiences for ages and even Hollywood with stories like the epic" The Ten Commandments" and "Prince of Egypt," constantly reminds us of the great works God did in bringing his word to Abraham to pass. But did you know where his greatest works of freeing slaves take place?

Right today! I was a slave of sin. Today I am free on my way to the millennium!

CHAPTER THREE
AS THE WORLD CONTINUES

As the years go by and the centuries go on. Everything changes. People change, medicine changes, technology changes, even the weather pattern changes. People never had snow, now they have snow. There are horrible hurricanes that wipe a whole city out. And people and animals are homeless and have to start all over again. The thing I don't understand is why they give these treacherous things names, like Hurricane Henry?

Then there's fires that are out of control. People are forced to find new places to relocate. Then there's earthquakes that destroyed many homes, businesses, and killed a lot of people. There was one earthquake that was so big it shook up 2 million people. It went from Idaho to Canada. Now the technology keeps changing and it's hard to keep up. They have this G5 power system and they say it is making people sick. Rumors and lies. We don't know what is the truth. Terrible fires that were so out of control more than once. It destroyed many homes, businesses, and people had to relocate. And the flooded waters damaged a lot of properties, homes, and businesses. Much damage has been done all over the world. Through horrible disasters from nasty weather conditions the world is getting crazier by the day. The Bible says there is nothing new under the sun. Now with these computers and cell phones you can do many tasks. It is hard to keep up because they keep on changing. Now the smartphone can help you alot. My friend said she doesn't have a smartphone. I said, "You mean you got a dumb phone?" Then we laughed. Sometimes people pretend to be someone they are not when you chat online. So you have to be very careful. Do not give real personal information. Keep yourself and your family safe. I was talking to four guys at one time. I don't know what they were after. So sometimes you can get someone just to chat. That's good if they are not trying to scam you or get something out of you.

It's pretty neat to meet people all over the world and you become friends. You could video chat with them too, then you could see each other. Sometimes you get guys who say they are in love with you and the whole time they are scamming you and trying to get money from you. Well it's very easy for me to say no because I am always broke. If I had the money I wouldn't give them the money because I don't know them. There was a fella that asked me to marry him. Then he asked for a huge amount of money to get him here to the United States. I said no way and no way I'm marrying him. I talked to another fella online. He was kind of possessive. I don't know what he was after. My mom thinks it was my home. The man thought I owned my own home. I was glad when I didn't have any contact with him any more. One Sunday he texted me when I just got out of church.

He asked, "Are you sure you are at church?" Accusing me of lying and being somewhere else. He was in a different country. Apparently he had a daughter and needed a wife for him and a mom for his daughter. I was not going to be that person. I felt relieved when I didn't have to deal with him anymore. I've had 2 young men ask me for $100.00.

One guy said can he borrow $100.00 and the other said can I give him $100.00, so now when they text I ignore them because I know their motives are not right. I have no time for such people. I then start chatting with a man that is a four star general so he says he is single and has a sixteen year old daughter. He says he is at camp if I could send him a few hundred dollars. I don't even know this guy. He said he only needs a few hundred. I told him I have no money, which was the truth. Then he said he did not know how to tell me I said tell me what? Then he said that he is falling in love with me. That he wants us to be together for the rest of our lives. I said I am in love with somebody else and am getting married soon. I have had a few guys video chat with me, on my cell phone. I did not answer. I did not want to talk with them or see them. But they kept on being persistent. I can be persistent also. Found out that when men try to get money or anything from you on the internet it's called catfishing."Guys will try to get you to buy them cards or get money or anything for their gain and your loss.So i haven't heard from my finance' in six months i figured we are done." I don't know what happened to him. If he died or what!"He asked me to wait for him until he got out of the navy which was only a few more months but I am not gonna wait around for a dead man."

After a year and a half I decided to move on with my life I met another man who is in the military who also is a widower. We began spending lots of time texting each other. I wondered if Jackson was his real name so I decided to ask him. I said is Jackson Michael your real name? His response was, is your name really your real name? I thought to myself it was good enough for me. Not too much longer Jackson asked me if I would give my heart to him. I said give it a little time if it's meant to be it will happen." No sooner had I said this, something inside of me began to feel strange." I felt all fluttery inside." And like I was in some kind of trance. My heart began to beat real hard and fast."I had to catch my breath a few times." I told Jackson to wait!" something is happening to me." I believe I am falling in love with you. I said it will happen to you too. Jackson said ``It already has. He said you are an answer to prayer." I prayed for a woman like you. He had a son aged 12 in a boarding school. He had no one to care for his son Alex I began to fall in love with this sweet man.`` I've heard of women coming out of bad relationships and finding a good and sweet man of their dreams. I wished in my heart that I could be blessed like them with a prince and knight of shining armour." I found my prince." I can't believe this is real." God is good all the time and all the time God is good.``We spent lots of time texting each other.I told him I had a blind eye. thinking he wouldn't want to be with me anymore. He said that I am God sent' he had prayed for me for years. and that he loves me unconditionally. And that I deserve to be pampered like a baby." That he would do everything in his power to make me happy." That it took him so long to find me." And that he couldn't afford to lose me."happy." I can't beliveIt's my time to be blessed.``Should I say our time to be blessed." God knew the desire of my heart." I desired another son. Because I did not get to raise my son all his years. Now my dreams are becoming real." Wow!" This is too good to be true!"overwhelming. and beautiful. This is real." It's our time now it's our time."

CHAPTER FOUR

LIFE GOES ON

Medicine has changed, so has sickness. Some animals are not being treated well. There are a lot of homeless animals, like people. Some dogs are being used to fight each other to the death. The men bet money on this. Shame how many mistreated God's creation.

Somebody took a video of a woman throwing newborn puppies in the river. They said I hope she gets caught. I hope she does too. Some crazy drivers ran over some geese. They were hit so hard that their body parts were scattered everywhere.

Some man stopped his car and got out to pick the geese mess up. He was very upset and yelled, "Who did this? This is wrong." Yes, this is wrong how animals are treated. They are God's creation. They are supposed to be here for our enjoyment. Not for us to hurt or harm them. This is sad. When my mom was a young girl she had gotten bit by a squirrel.

Then she got Scarlet Fever. Today we don't hear of Scarlet Fever, or Leprosy disease, which I've heard is called Hansen disease now and is treatable. The mumps, very rare measles. Today we hear of other diseases, such as AIDs, kidney disease, cancer, heart attack, diabetes, Parkinson's, multiple sclerosis, polio, Arthritis, pneumonia, strep throat, strokes,hepatitis,Muscle Disc Free, and many other diseases and other illnesses. They don't have a cure for. And many I have never heard of or could even pronounce the name. But they are working very hard to keep patients as comfortable as they possibly can. I know that it doesn't seem like nobody cares, nobody understands. There is only so much a person can do.

CHAPTER FIVE
WE NEED A REVIVAL

We need a spiritual waking up. We need to get a hold of God and not let him go. When things are fine, we don't forget about him. Or just come to him and ask for things. We need our eyes opened wide and see what the Lord wants us to see. And not just what we want to see.

Now the whole world is shaken up. There is tragedy all over the world. There are killings, there is war, there is bad weather for alot of countries and states. In fact, I have a friend that moved to a different state. Opened a bakery then a flood destroyed everything that she just built up. Unbelievable. I felt sad for my friend. It's like the whole world was getting a wake up call from God. It just felt like everything was going out of control. Everybody was suffering in one way or another. If it wasn't sickness, it was finances, if it wasn't that it was a loss of a loved one. If not that it was damage to their home or business or both.

People needed God more than they thought they needed him. Thing is we come to God when we are broken and weary. What about when everything is okay? This is another scripture that is a blessing and you can apply it to your life. Philippians:3-14 I press on toward the goal unto the prize of the high calling of God in Christ Jesus. Let us therefore be perfect. Be thus minded wise minded this also God shall also reveal to you. Only where you have attained. You see we need a revival in our hearts, in our minds, in our body and in our spirits. We need to be regenerated and on fire. Don't let your light go out! Instead let it shine. After all, we are little Christs. And we represent the Lord. 2 Timothy 3:1-5. There will be terrible times in the last days, people will be lovers of themselves, Boastful,proud,abusive,disobedient to their parents.

Ungrateful,unholy,without love,unforgiving, slanderous, without self control, brutal, not lovers of the good. Treacherous, rash, conceited. Lovers of pleasures, rather than lovers of God. Having a form of Godliness but denying its power. Having nothing to do with such people. Now this generation does not care much to have respect, or wanting to work hard. Of course this really depends on how you were raised and what kind of morals you were taught. And if you believe in them and keep them. To pass on down to your grandchildren, \and each generation keeps it going. Nothing wrong with sharing and keeping a good thing in the family. Something to be proud of. This is a good quality, Good morals.

CHAPTER SIX

THE WORLD, IS IN A CHAO'S

Great," now there is some virus going around that started in China. The Coronavirus; covid-19. The whole world is affected. The virus is spreading quickly all over the world. Millions of people have the virus. It is spreading quickly. From state to state. In Italy people were dying by the thousands a day. In China, they were dying by the thousands a day. All the Hospitals are running out of supplies.

1.28 million hit with the Coronavirus and rising by the minute. There's not enough equipment, or supplies. It would cost 2 trillion dollars to supply all the medical supplies and equipment we need to treat the people and give them the proper care they need. The U of M loses more than 3 million dollars. Businesses are closed down. Everybody suffers in one way or another. New York had more than 55,000.00 cases and rising. There are some people that are frantic. 450,000.00 million for food banks. There are some people that are terrified, some people are angry so they stay mad at everybody and everything. It's best to keep your distance from them. Speaking of keeping your distance, we are told to wear masks and to keep 6 feet away from each other. Lines of people wait their turn to go into the store to buy items. Tape is on the floor at the stores to keep people distant 6 feet from one another because they were only allowing a few at a time as a precaution as to not getting the virus. This is a living nightmare and day mare. The little dairy farms were asked to slow down their process of intake of milk and eggs because everything has shut down. All the schools were canceled. Self distancing is on the rise. Non-essential stores and businesses mandated to close. Parks, trails, entire cities locked up.Entire sports season was canceled. The Tennis Championship hasn't been canceled since World War two. Concerts, tours, festivals, entertainment events, canceled. Weddings, family celebrations, holiday gatherings, canceled. No gatherings. Churches are closed. No gatherings of 6 people or more. Don't socialize with anyone outside of your home. Children's outdoor play parks are closed. All the pools, beaches, and fishing are closed. Wisconsin had to pour out gallons and gallons of milk because of the restaurants being closed. People lost their jobs. People can't pay their bills. So a lot of people are suffering from this pandemic.

100's of thousands of people are out of work because of this pandemic. 26 million people applied for unemployment. The president is giving everyone a stimulus check to help us through this tough time. It's not enough but at least it is something to help a little. I think when this virus is gone we will feel the pain for a while. It will take a long time to get over because we lost a lot of lives and we still are. This is sad because there's not a whole lot we can do about it until they find a cure for this evil virus. So we just wait again. There's that word again, "Wait." I don't like that word too much because I have to keep learning it over and over. I have to use it all the time. I have to practice it all the time. I know it will take a lot longer to get over this pandemic of crisis.Voices from the pandemic is an oral history of covid-19 and those affected. Landlords, apartment owners and housing industry groups have unleashed a barrage of legal challenges against the Trump administration's order protecting renters from eviction, leaving millions of families homeless in the middle of a pandemic over the past month. Lawyers and Lobbyists have undated federal, state and local courts. They have sought to stop renters from invoking the federal ban. And in some cases they've tried to squash the policy altogether arguing that the government did not have the authority to issue it in the first place.

Many landlords are upset with the governor doing this.

My daughter happens to be one, she is a single parent that worked hard to get to where she is at and the people living in her apartment building owe her 8000,00 dollars and there's nothing she can do about it. The sad thing is the people that live there own their own business they are just taking advantage of what the governor said.

So sad how many people are dishonest and nothing can be done about it. It's wrong, it's not fair but then again life is not fair. My daughter wrote a letter to the governor. I doubt it will make any difference who knows if he reads his letters or if he even gets them.That's sad if he doesn't care enough to read what's on people's hearts or does he think all we do is complain. If we don't address the issue how is he going to know.what can he do about it? That's the question: how can he make dishonest people be honest? He can't. It's a sad situation.

Amazon says more than 9000,00 have covid-19

Ten reported states had their highest numbers in new coronavirus cases. Here's how every major workforce has been impacted by the coronavirus pandemic Employee paid-time off policies.are being revised. Many workers at many US companies are being instructed to work from home. Stores,offices, factories, are shut down temporarily and venues other workplaces and venues change. There were already fundamental shifts in the workforce as new technologies in the workplace started. The covid-19 pandemic accelerated these changes at a nearly unimaginable pace. The work force is rewired as tailored news and information specifically for employers and executives to keep track of what companies are doing with regard to their workforce. To Help leaders navigate through these unprecedented times. wire is tailored news and information.

CHAPTER SEVEN

QUALITY CHECK

How much time do we spend with our loved ones? When we get a day off. Are we too tired and too busy to meet the needs of our family? The boys want to go outside and throw the football around. Your little girl wants you to read to her. Your wife wants to go on a date. You say you are too tired. It's your only day off, you just need time for yourself. Thing is we are not guaranteed tomorrow. Yesterday is gone, today is here, tomorrow may or may not come for you. So take each day just as if it is your last day here on earth and make the best of it as you can, because spending good quality time with your loved ones will always be important. And in time, it turns into only a memory. To Be treasured. And nothing can measure up to that. You will never regret it. But you will regret it if you didn't spend time with them. In the end your time will be well spent. It will be something you will cherish forever. Because you will never get that chance or that day again. It will be gone. Now if you are not feeling well, there's not much you can do.

Just make it the best you can. Same as if you are tired and rather be by yourself. You will be blessed by blessing somebody's else's day. I promise you, you wouldn't want it any other way. When you make time for your loved ones everyone is happier You all benefit from family time maybe you don't have much time at least have the time to sit and have a meal and talk or listen this means the world to your family that you care and that you are there for them let them know they don't ever have to be afraid to come to you for advice questions,whatever,that you won't judge them,because that's not your job it's the Lord's.The Lord's alone. Coming from a dysfunctional household doesn't mean you have to stay that way. You can learn new habits, good habits, that you can teach your own family. "Be careful who you go around. There have been 15,000 new hires to pharmacy technicians needed for the flu season and covid-19 presence. Cruise ship rescues 24 people from a boat off the Florida coast. There have been over a million reported new cases of coronavirus in a 2 week period. The whole city may have to be on a lock down. Not only our city, many cities. A little girl trapped under earthquake rubble for 65 hours rescued 2 children in Turkey as the quake death toll reached 81. The Stillwater correctional facility was placed on a lock down due to covid 19 outbreak in the incarcerated population. According to the Minnesota department of corrections the outbreak is currently limited to two living units and the medical was supplemented to prevent spread to other populations,out of living unit programming and work activities have been suspended in- unit daily programming is limited to small groups. Additionally meals, and medications are being delivered to the cells. And medical care is being delivered in units when possible.The Duration of the lockdown is dependent on further tests results. It's expected to last 14 days.750 inmates have the covid-19 infection. 150 employees have the infection. One man has died; they did not release his name hoping no more people die. When will this nightmare be over with? We just have to trust God that he will bring us through this and that he said he would never leave us or forsake us. We have to trust in his word because his word is true and real and alive. We have to believe if you doubt then ask God for more faith and he will give it to you because he wants you to have faith. Freely ask freely he will give. For now we wait for the outcome of the presidential campaign. Biden is ahead of Trump for now. Trump says there is voting fraud that he wants to recount in a few states. Apparently there were cameras that caught some suspicious activities. In fact they caught a woman voting in one state then went to another to vote again. So much talk we don't know what to believe. I know one thing this campaign is draganing on and everybody is tired of it. We want it to be over just like the coronavirus. We are tired of it and we want it to go away.

    The world is getting shaken, The weather is getting out of control with the hurricane's, the earthquakes, the floods, the fires, the tornadoes, the winds are really out of control. People are in panic because the storms in some places have left most of them homeless. And businesses, there is nothing. They have to rebuild their city, towns, and countries. They are grateful they have each other. And for someone you don't know to give you a hug and give you a smile and say everything's gonna be okay. When people gather together to help one another you can feel the love, concern, and you trust these people you don't even know. This helps you feel that you are somebody and that you do matter. And that somebody cares. Then you don't feel so all alone because you're not. And each day will get better and you will get stronger and things won't be so hard anymore because you are somebody. And you matter. And God loves you.

CHAPTER EIGHT

GO WITH THE FLOW

There is a shortage of masks, gowns, and gloves for our front line workers. They showed on the news two women fighting over toilet paper. They were really going at it. Shortage of ventilators, for the critically ill. Panic buying sets in and we have no toilet paper. No disinfecting supplies, no paper towels. No laundry soap, no hand sanitizer. The shelves are bare at the stores. So you have to go and hunt for some toilet paper. It may take all day. And you don't know how far you're going to have to go to finally find some toilet paper. But you're not alone. So when you find some, be sure to tell the others, so they can stop hunting. Manufacturers, dilleries and other businesses switch their lines. Government closes the border to all non-essential travel. Fines are established for breaking rules. The Mall of America opened up so they could use the space for blood donors. There is a shortage of blood at the red cross. So you make an appointment and take your turn. It's pretty spacey at the Mall of America and the hospitals. Stadiums and recreation facilities open up for overflow of covid-19 patients. Press conferences from the President daily. And the Governess updates on news cases daily on the recoveries and deaths. Government incentives to stay at home. People being caught doing activities with more than six people will get a ticket. A woman told me there were a lot of people out at Harriet Island. They didn't get tickets. Well, that's why this is not slowing down because people are not following the rules. They are not staying home. The thing is, it affects all of us. Not just the people breaking the rules. This is sad. Some nursing homes have been affected. Positive of having the Coronavirus. Ninety percent of the people that were tested had the virus. A young man that went to visit his grandmother often, was not allowed to go visit her anymore. So he stood outside her window and talked to her on the phone. That was a way they could see each other. Some of the nursing homes, and living situations were closed to any visitors. The people that lived in these places, for a little while, were doing activities in the hallway. Everybody stood by their apartment door so we made sure we stood six feet away from each other. We played Bingo and the girls talked on the microphone so everyone could hear. I won one game. Then a woman got the virus that lived a few doors down from me. Then we stopped doing activities in the hall and had to isolate ourselves again. While we are in quarantine, we are like prisoners. Not able to leave our apartment. We couldn't even go out in the hall. We didn't even get to see our neighbors. We didn't get to go check our mail, we didn't get to go do our laundry. We were totally isolated from the whole world. Now if the sun shined, that made our day because being isolated and having it dark and grey did not go good together. We didn't get to go down to the dinning room to eat. We got our food served to us. If it was gray and dark outside, that just made you feel more down, more alone, more depressed. We have had too many gray days this winter already. Now we know how our grandparents felt when we didn't go visit them. They were all alone and forgotten. Also our elderly parents, because we were too busy and we didn't make the time. Life is short. Shorter than you think. As far as the nursing homes go, the elderly are mis-treated. They are being thrown out of the nursing homes like a piece of trash. Nursing homes in the U.S. are evicting vulnerable residents to make more room for more profitable Coronavirus patients. This happened in group homes for the developmentally disabled as well. It's all about the money. We must implement more home based waivers so they can stay in their own homes. They have been doing this for decades long before this virus hit. Medical care in the U.S. is about making profits, not caring about people. Nursing homes take residents to the emergency room and want to give their bed away so that they can admit more profitable people. These places are required to follow government guidelines. Why are they allowed to break rules? It's called money, that's why.

CHAPTER NINE

GETTING CORONAVIRUS

A friend got the virus. She didn't stay home. She paid the consequences. She recovered. Thank God. This is her interpretation of what she went through. When you get sick from coronavirus, you will have a fever, the highest fever you've ever had in your life to breathe slowly. It's not going to be like your typical flu and fevers.

You're going to breathe slowly, like you've had a sponge stuck in your nose. When you try to fill your lungs with air heavily by inhaling, you will still feel like you are out of breath. And that will scare you. You are going to cough a lot, so much that you're going to tire until you almost pass out. Every time you do it your chest, arms, back, fingers, and toes will hurt. You will try to catch air through your nose and you will not be able to so they are going to give you oxygen. And it's going to burn the entrance of your nose. That is going to hurt even more. And if you can't breathe another Doctor will come in and put in a couple of half tubes to get past bronchi and into the lungs. That is called an artificial respirator. It is really disturbing and annoying. And on top of that you cannot speak or eat. You will be alone in a closed room. You will not be able to see your partner, your mother, your father, or your children that you love so much. Or any other family members. Because you are going to affect them with the same thing that is killing you. You will feel so alone that you will start to cry. And you will be afraid of dying. You will think of the ones you love and you will cry even more. That will worsen everything, hence shortness of breath. This is when you will understand. This is why they told you to stay at home. Stay home and save lives. Global confirmed cases: 2,699338 that have recovered. Deaths 188,437 and still climbing. Very sad, very devastating. Very real. In 1986, David Wilkerson prophesied that a plague was coming into the world. And the bars, churches, and government will shut down. The plague will hit New York and shake it. Like it never was shaken. The plague is going to force prayerless believers, into radical prayer and into their Bibles. And repentance will be the cry from the men of God in the pulpit. And out of it will come a third great awakening. That will sweep America and the world. A few years back president Obama said we were going to have a pandemic. They knew it back then and did nothing about it and the republicans and democrats say they are for the people! Hmmm. Hundreds of college football players have been tested for the Coronavirus, most have been positive. What do we do now? Wait until next season to play college football? The NFL recommends that some sideline players wear masks. A rare ring of fire solar eclipse on the longest day of the year it's an astronomical miracle. There have been none in at least a hundred years. But the ring of fire eclipse that falls in mid summer weather in the northern or southern hemisphere is even more in common. My daughter says to me to open up your windows. I said "no." My niece told me not to because the Coronavirus is in the air. My daughter says as long as I am not with any people. I said no, I would be the one out of a million that Corona came to visit. My daughter started laughing. Now I do keep the window open every chance that it is nice out and you don't have to have the air on or not raining. My cat likes to sit up on the ledge and look out the window. It's cute to watch him. Well now they are talking about space age flying that could change flying forever. It looks like a spaceship, runs on fuel that's up until a few years ago experts were calling crazy and has barely left the drawing board, but in the eyes of one of the world's leading aircrafts manufacturers it's undoubtedly the future, not even the distant future. Airbus hopes well to be soaring into the skies on one of it's radical new designs in just 15 years. Leaving the days of jet pollution and flight shaming behind us. The blended wing aircraft is one of a trinity-of eco-friendly hydrogen-fueled models unveiled recently by Airbus as part of its ambitions to spearhead the decarbonization of the aviation industry. It's a bold plan, and one that just a few short months ago might have seemed fanciful as demand for fossil fuel-powered air travel continued to rise, apparently immune to growing environmental concerns. But the arrival of covid-19 and its impact on aviation could've inadvertently cleared a flight path or opportunity for efforts to rethink the technology of getting the world up into the air. Airbus has baptized it's new program ZEROE. The designs revealed aren't the photo types but a starting point to explore. The tech needed in order to start building the first climate commercial planes. England lockdown may be longer than December, maybe extended. Authorities shut down a large indoor halloween party with nearly 400 hundred guests. Over 387 people violated coronavirus related emergencies orders. In attending the illegal bar/party,"and nine organizers were charged with multiple demeanors. Europs covid-19 cases doubled in five weeks total in infections surpassing 10 million just last month both latin america and Asia reported over ten million cases. With rapidly accelerating outbreaks.With 10% of the world's population, Europe counts for 23%of the global caseload of 46.3 million in infections, death toll of nearly 1.2 million lives the surging cases France, Germany and the united kingdom have announced nationwide lockdowns for at least the next month that are almost as strict as in March and April. Portugal has imposed a partial lock down. Spain and Italy are tightening restrictions. Europe has reported more than 1.6 million cases in the past seven days. Nearly half the 3.3 million reported worldwide,with over 16,100 deaths, a 44% jump over the previous week. For every 10,000 people over 127 coronavirus have been reported there have been 278 cases per 10,000 residents within the region, Eastern Europe has one third of the total reported covid-19 cases the highest number of deaths with about 32% of coronavirus deaths according to annysis. Russia is the worst affected eastern European country with over 1.6 million covid-19 cases infections. The nation's deputy prime minister said that hospital beds were at 90% capacity in 16 regions of the country. I had a friend that I grew up with who died of coronavirus, hard to believe.

CHAPTER TEN
ONE DAY AT A TIME

Everyday is a new day
and different from the day before.
Each day is made special
for the unique person you are,
so treasure each day in it's own way
because you will never see it again
and in the end
it will never end.

I think things are slowing down a bit. I am glad when the sun does shine, I always say the sun is smiling at us when it does shine. Things do seem to be a little calmer than when we first heard about the virus. They say it was developed by a scientist in China and from there it took off. I don't understand why somebody would want to create something bad? Silly me, it probably was not meant for bad. It just turned out that way by accident.Everybody has different theories of how it was started or why it was started. It sure traveled fast and killed lots of people. Some people are taking advantage of using those masks for the wrong reason. Some guy just got robbed of his phone money from somebody who had the mask on. Now he can't pay his bill. Hopefully it won't be too much longer and this will be all over. We will get through this as we have everything else that has been thrown at us. "We will prevail"

In Romans 8:28 one of my favorite scriptures. And we know all things work together for the good to them that love God to them are called according to his purpose. Now I know there are lots of scriptures that we can look up and read and meditate or study to receive comfort. Or get answers, wisdom, or whatever it may be. Looking to Jesus and his word really is the answer to everything. Because Jesus is bigger and better than any Coronavirus pandemic covid-19 any time. He said he would never leave us or forsake us. Even when we are going through hardships and it seems like he's not listening to us. He is right beside us, giving us encouragement and praise that you are standing like a true trooper. And that you are not giving up. You are going to reach your goals. And see your dreams and desires come to pass. And that he will be right there with you. You are not alone. It's going to be alright. It will all work out. May you take a new grip with your tired hands and mark out a straight path for your feet. God has given you promises to hang on to, and enough light for the road in front of you. You have what you need to stand in faith and embrace joy. Tell your soul that the devil will not stand in the way of God's promises. Remember that he has no power to steal your purpose from you! The Lord himself fights for you. So take your stand, hold your ground, and refuse to be bullied by your fears. Jesus won the war so you can win this battle. You are mighty in God my friend! Hewbrews 10:12-13: So be made strong even in your weakness, for as you keep walking forward on God's paths an offering he has perfected.

CHAPTER ELEVEN

A GLOBAL CRISIS

Since the outbreak of Coronavirus, there have been multiple conspiracy theories about how the virus has been created. In a lab now a forward, a company video, is being shared on social media. To prove that the theory was right. Although the novel Coronavirus outbreak started in China's Wuhan, in December most of the cases now are from around the world. And it continues to spread. India has more than 2,300 active cases as of April 3rd. We need science to save the day, not panic and fake news. We really need to trust God to get us through this storm as he has many others. He said he would never leave us or forsake us. We have to trust in his word. Trust in him. We will be alright! I am so glad the Lord is patient and slow to anger with us because If he was not perfect none of us probably would be here. Look what we have done to his creation and he still keeps forgiving us over and over. What about the people in Sweden, getting chips inside of their hands. They will use that chip to buy and sell things. All their information is on that chip. Is this really a sign of the end times? A few people had this on Facebook and in a few different versions. Eternal Father, you made the whole world stop spinning for a while. You silenced the noise that we have created. You made us bend our knees again and ask for a miracle. You closed your churches so that we would realize how dark our world is without you in it. You humble the proud and the powerful. The economy is crashing, businesses are closing. We thought that everything we have and everything we possess was the result of our hard work. When in fact we need to humble ourselves. We have forgotten it was always your grace and mercy that made us who we are. Amen," There are tornadoes, hurricanes, floods, the worst fires, in history. Viruses going around the world. And people are still fighting to keep God out of everything. In the schools Christmas is called winter break. Easter is called spring break. And what about prayer in school? Shouldn't we be allowed to pray to bless our food? Or just pray in peace if we want? Seems to me God is sending a message loud and clear to put God back where he belongs! Amen! It has been reported that more than 7 million cases of Coronavirus have been reported. When will it all end? Nobody knows but the father. As if everyday people die from cancer, car accidents, and now coronavirus. We have been living our lives like we will be on earth forever. Like there's no heaven. Maybe these trials are our mercy in disguise. Maybe this virus is actually God's way of purifying us and cleansing our soul and bringing us back to him. Only the father knows. Trump says he is going to cut off food stamps for 700,000 Americans. Federal Judge strikes down Trump's plan to slash food stamps for 700,000 Americans. Republicans and Democrats have been sparring for a month now about a new deal some of the programs passed through in the spring. Including the federal $600 weekly supplements to workers who lost jobs-have expired. President Trump recently said that he could support even more than the white house's latest 1.88 trillion proposal, though it isn't clear senate Republicans would get behind. Saturday night after the conversation there were differences that needed to be worked through. Biden and his son got paid 100 million dollars and ten million of that went to Joe Biden for helping the chinese communist party. Unemployment remains high. Travel industry remains in ruff shape. And there are growing concerns about problems in the commercial real estate sector. Many restaurants are still struggling, and some continue to go out of business. Seven months after the pandemic floored the American economy. The Senate and secretary continue to haggle over the contours of a deal as part of negotiations that have stretched on for months. It was highly uncertain if they would be able to reach a resolution where the senate cited progress in talks but also criticized the administration for partly rejecting democrats' nationally testing proposal. Democrats have also demanded more funding for childcare, and tax credits for families. The legislation expected on the floor Tuesday would provide an additional $260.00 billion to small business paycheck protection programs and allow businesses that already got loans this year Be able to receive funding. Mcconnell will try to advance an approximately$600 billion bill that will include jobless benefits for the unemployed, funding for schools and health care systems, and new small businesses funding. But will exclude many provisions sought by Democrats and Trump, including a new round of $ 1,200 stimulus checks. What to look for in the final 2020 presidential Debate Trump and Biden will face off for the last time before election day. Millions of voters who skipped 2016 aren't sitting out this election. A record number of women of color are running for congress. More than 40 million Americans have already voted with 13 days left until election day. The still water correctional facility was placed on lockdown due to covid-19 outbreak in the incarcerated population.According to the Minnesota Department of Corrections the outbreaks are currently to two living units and the medical was implemented to prevent spread to other populations. Out of living unit programming and work activities have been suspended, in- unit daily programming is limited to small groups. Additionally meals, and medications are being delivered to the cells. And medical care is being delivered to the units when possible. The duration is dependent on further test results. It's expected to last 14 days. 750 inmates have gotten the virus and 150 employees have gotten the virus. There has been one death but they would not release the man's identity. Hoping no more would die. St. Cloud Correctional facility is the oldest facility there is; it was built in 1889 four officers were injured after an inmate assaulted an officer in the dining hall. The Minnesota Department of Corrections has announced that in person visits will be suspended at all facilities for a minimum of two weeks. According to the disease division director. Prisons, and jails have a unique population with many people living in close quarters. Actions such as limiting visitors" are reasonable in this situation" We are working to ensure the safety of our staff,the safety of those in the facilities,and ongoing delivery of essential services including food, water and health services in the worst case scenario of an outbreak in any facility. The Doc is exploring ways to expand the availability of electronic visiting, or potential reduction of waiver fees." Little by little things are getting taken away from us until we have nothing left to enjoy for pleasure,it's almost as if we are being grounded and until something changes we can't get things back. Now for this pandemic the people that don't follow the rules are making it hard for everyone. Maybe that's why this pandemic won't go away. But we all have to suffer the consequences. It's too bad but that's the way it goes. People aren't dying as much as they were everyday. In the beginning when this pandemic first started. Some people are still being careful and following the rules and guidelines and then there are those who just don't care. My sister went to wal-mart to pick up my mother's prescriptions,and she said there were a few people in the store that were not wearing masks,so she told the employees at the door, she should have told them that if they don't wear a mask then they can't shop in the store in fact there should be a sign saying if you don't wear a mask in the store then you can't come in. That's fair but of course i don't think they would want to chase customers away. People should follow rules, some people would say that's why there are rules so we can break them. I've heard that said before. It takes all kinds.

CHAPTER TWELVE

A WAKE UP CALL

Maybe we are getting things shut down and people are dying and people are so sick and maybe the men of God who are crying out to God is what God is calling all of us to do. Maybe we need to do a spiritual examination. Because this is all so creepy to happen. It is not normal and we don't know how to fix it. No scientist, no Doctor, nobody can fix this, only God. And so while men are working on a cure for this deadly disease people are dying everyday. People are getting the virus everyday and all we can do is pray and wait on God to bring us some kind of relief. We have no idea when that will be. It could be a year or longer we don't know. We will try whatever is available to help us because we are desperate. Worried for our loved ones to not get this or even ourselves. All we can do is pray. And wait on the Lord to see what happens next. If we get some kind of cure because now we are getting everything taken away. It's for a reason. It's almost as if we are being disciplined for our behavior and maybe we are. Getting things taken away like we have things shutting down. But the dying part I don't understand. I guess we are not supposed to understand. We can't figure God out anyhow. We are just to trust that he knows what's best for us. Maybe the world was too crowded and we needed space for the newborn babies. Only God knows why all those people died from Coronavirus. People are still dying. God holds the present, the future, the past and remembers the past no more. I am sure we can trust him for a breakthrough when the time is right. It's hard, we get anxious and we want things done right now. Then we have to be taught another lesson in the process. There you go, we never stop learning. At least we got the best teacher in the world, Jesus Christ! He is the same today as he was yesterday and will be forever more Amen! When we do get a vaccine for the virus covid-19 many parents are hesitant to have their kids take the shot. But if schools require this it will be a huge issue. I don't think most people understand that yet. Schools are likely to require students to get the covid-19 vaccines in the future, potentially setting the stage for a showdown between reluctant parents and education officials. Eleven Minnesota schools experiencing covid-19 outbreaks. 150-Million could fall into extreme poverty due to covid-19 pandemic. Doctors and nurses battle virus skeptics. 34 people tested positive for covid-19 in the Whitehouse. Doctors find coronavirus in the brains of cadavers. Doctors, and health experts question Trump's plans to resume activities. Meanwhile Hurricane Delta makes landfall in Louisiana as a category 2 storm. Heavy rain gusty winds continue as Delta remnants and the system continues to move northeast past tropical cyclone Delta's center over northern Mississippi this morning as of 4:30 am. Several flood alerts remain in place for parts of Georgia, South Carolina and North Carolina near Atlanta. Georgia received heavy storms overnight. There were six reports of tornadoes in north Georgia including reports of downed trees. Atlanta is reporting 2-4 inches of rain in White county. Georgia is resulting in flash flood warnings. Early in the morning Delta is expected to bring gusty and rainy conditions to the south today, then reach the New York City metro area including a Hail watch. A Hail warning is issued through Monday evening as winds gusts could top 40 mph. Up to four inches of rain are possible through Monday night In portions of the DelMarva area and central New Jersey. While California is setting up for another week of potentially critical fire weather with hot dry dusty conditions all the way to the end of the work week. As I said, one part of the world is drowning and the other is burning. Will we ever get a break? Update: Dozens killed in floods across southeast Asia as tropical storm approaches. Two dozen emergency calls including high water rescues in areas were outer bands where the storm hit like Baton Rouge, earlier than expected on Friday. The Delta is on the verge of becoming a tropical depression. The storm remains a concern as it tracks across Mississippi leaving nearly 800,000 people without power. The storm winds flipped two trucks over on their sides on the interstate between Lake Charles and Lafayette Louisiana. Delta is still bringing damaging winds in hundreds of miles in getting lots of land reports of lots of trees and power poles down. Gust over 50 mph. Are common near the lowest pressure, now over east LA. And western MS Delta is the

25th name of the 2020 Atlantic hurricane season. It's also the 10th named storm this season to make landfall in the continental US, setting the record for the most storms in one year. Delta is the 7th major storm to hit the gulf coast since June. The storm first made landfall at a category 2 storm about 20 miles south of Cancun, Mexico early Wednesday before hitting Yucatan, Pennsylvania. Delta transformed into a category 4 hurricane over the course of 30 hours increasing its speed to nearly 100 mph. At that time one forecaster said he could not find any previous record of an Allylic storm escalating that quickly or strongly. This is how they rate the hurricanes: Category 1: is very dangerous. Winds will produce some damage. Winds range from 74 to 95 mph. Falling debris could strike people, livestock and pets. Older mobile homes could be destroyed. Protected glass windows will generally make it through the hurricane without major damage. Frame homes, apartments and shopping centers may experience some damage. Snapped power lines could result in short term power outages.

Category 2: hurricanes: There is a bigger risk of injury or death to people, livestock and pets from flying debris. Older mobile homes will likely be destroyed and debris can destroy newer mobile homes too. Frame homes, apartment buildings, and shopping centers may see major roof and siding damage and many trees will be uprooted. Residents should expect near total power loss after category 2 hurricanes, with outages lastings anywhere from a few days to a few weeks. Category 3: Winds range from 111 to 129 pmh. There is a high risk of injury or death to people, livestock and pets from flying and falling debris. Nearly all mobile homes will be destroyed and most new ones will experience major damage. The storm will uproot many trees and may block roads. Electricity and water will likely be unavailable for several days to a few weeks after the storm. Category 4: Wind will blow most windows out on high rise buildings, uproot most trees, and will likely take down many power lines. Power outages can last for weeks or even months after storms of this level. Water shortages are also common in the aftermath of category 4 hurricanes, potentially making the affected area uninhabitable for weeks or months. Category 5: the highest category. The winds are 157 mph or higher. People, livestock, and pets can be in danger from flying debris, even indoors. Most mobile homes will be completely destroyed, and a high percentage of frame homes will be destroyed. Commercial buildings with wood roofs will experience severe damage. Metal buildings may collapse and high rise windows will be nearly all blown out. Category 5 is likely to uproot most trees and ruin most power poles. Like category 4, power outages can be expected to last for weeks to months. People should expect long term water shortages as well. Only 3 hurricanes have made landfall as a category 5 since 1924. One of the most famous hurricanes in recent decades is Hurricane Andrew back in 1992. Hurricane Camille was a category 5 when it in 1969 as was 1930's Labor Day hurricane. Category 6: There is no such thing as a category 6 hurricane, When hurricane Irma was headed towards the coast of

Southern Florida in August it had wind speeds of 185 mph, according to the New York Times but the Simpson's scale only goes up to 5. Some people have been talking about creating a category 6 hurricane but a category means total destruction. So, while there is a difference between 151 to 200 mph there may be no practical difference. The problem with hurricane category is the Simpson scale only takes into account a storm's maximum wind speed and disregards other threats like rainfall and storm surge. Even a category 1 hurricane can bring serious damage and risk to life and limb. People in their path may underestimate the damage they pose because of the Simpson scale. An alternative of the Simpson scale is Accuweather, which takes in other metrics besides wind speed into account. Meanwhile, over 11,500 firefighters are still in the front lines of 21 wildfires across the state. 13 of those are the main major incidents of a fire. A weather watch is in effect for most of northern California due to low humidity and gust winds starting the weather is expected to continue to friday. Residents can expect breezy conditions with gusts around 20-25 mph dry conditions and above normal temperatures. Since the start of the year over 8,500 wildfires have burned over the total number of fatalities statewide is 31 and more than 9,200 structures have been destroyed. Health officials have forecast an air quality index of 55 for Tuesday in the sacramento region, which is moderate. Colorado wildfire grows into largest in state history. Left vulnerable by conditions,more than 30,000 have burned in what so far has been one of the worst years ever. In the state a woman was driving to her home in the Colorado mountains on Saturday when she saw ominous plumes swirling in the sky. In an instant this woman's mind went back to the year 2013 the last time she had been forced out by nature. Her home had been destroyed as was much of Jamestown. The 280-person community where she lives. Then the worst flood in a generation. This time it was swiftly growing wildfire at the end of a long and brutal season that had her packing to leave the house she had rebuilt and moved in just four months earlier. her heart was beating fast"as she recalled fleeing the flood with a single suitcase that she happened to have packed for her son's wedding. Her breathing was shallow. She had to keep reminding herself to breathe. The fire started on Saturday at the woodlands near JamesTown, a late arrival in a season that would normally be nearing its end but still rages in Colorado straining fire fighting, resolving to their limit and signaling for scientists for another devastating consequence of rising temperatures in changing climate.

CHAPTER THIRTEEN

A GREAT AWAKENING

33 Million people have now filed for jobless aid in the seven weeks since the Coronavirus began.

Forcing millions of companies to close their doors and slash work forces. There are restaurants that are closing their doors for good. So sad. Because some of these restaurants I grew up knowing my whole life like Perkins, they were the only restaurant open 24 hours a day on Robert street. That was nice to go to other than white castles open 24 hours a day. And Baker's square closed down. How sad.

Now whenever we go by the empty buildings I feel saden, for all the damage that this pandemic has caused and still is causing. Can't wait for this to be over. I know I am not the only one. Whenever we go out in public we are advised to wear a mask at all times. Now the black folks don't want to wear them because of the profile it gives them. They are a target for the police. Or any redneck person that has hate. There was a young black man jogging. Two racist men, a father and son that were rednecks.

They saw him and decided to chase after him. When they caught up to him they shot the young man twice for no reason. The young man was only 25 years old. This young man hasn't begun to live his life yet. And apparently it was short lived. What these men did was wrong. Let there be justice for this young man's family. The young man's family is having a walkathon to bring justice to the family that did wrong to that young man. This is supposed to be an awakening, not only for our bodies but for our hearts, eyes, souls, minds, spirits. Now for a little boy to be afraid of a doll because the parents let him see a spooky movie of a doll is so sad. The parents should have had some discernment. I have a China hutch filled with dolls of different nationalities. When my youngest grandson comes over I have to put a sheet over the China hutch so he can't see the dolls. Now how sad is that. The owner of a salon got put in jail because he opened his salon when we were still having the lock down. Now they say the state fair is canceled. I am glad I was hoping that it would be canceled because our health is far more important than to get another outbreak of the virus. And this is what the government said as well. They say that the lock down will be extended to the end of summer.

They keep changing the date. Everything is upside down. It feels like fall weather and we are locked up like prisoners. The sun hardly shines. That's how it was all winter, gray and dark. The only sunshine we have is Jesus. He is the truth, the way, the light!

CHAPTER FOURTEEN
A SHIELD OF PROTECTION

The world is changing. The world is not ending. The world is just crazy and so are the people in it. The government made the announcement that a few things can open up for the public. But we still need to take precaution. We still need to wear masks. We still need to wash our hands frequently. We still need to keep the limit on people gathering together to a minimum of 8-10 to be safe. There was a woman that came to live in my building. She only lived a couple doors down from me. She found out that she had the covid-19 virus. She did not know that she had been sick for quite some time. I was in the elevator with her, just her and I. It's a miracle I didn't get it because usually I catch what other people have. I kept wondering how my neighbour was doing. Then I found out she had died. Wow! One minute they are here, the next minute they are gone. It was in the paper that her family is trying to raise funds for her tombstone. How sad. If I had the money I would pay for it for them even though she's not family. I guess you can say she's family because she is a child of God and he is our father. She didn't live long in our apartment building. Only a few months. She did say she had a daughter. I will pray for her family. They will need strength and grace from the Lord. Only the Lord can give these things. That they desperately need now.

God said he would never leave us or forsake us. Hebrews 13:5 says, let your conversation be without covetousness; As I will never leave you or forsake you. He stays true to his word. Now another disease has been found to come on the younger generation ages 21 and under. 3 children have died so far. Apparently you get a high fever and swollen parts of the body also purplish color skin. The disease and control centers are trying to find out what it is before more kids die. Now this seems like we are in a roller coaster ride of bad stops of virus, sickness, illnesses, and diseases. Germany hits a record of almost 20,000, new cases. We can't live freely or we can't live in peace if we have to be on guard all the time. Well that's the way it is for now. It won't be this way forever. We have to think positive because if we don"t then we will let the devil steal our joy. I don't want to give him that pleasure. Besides, the battle belongs to the Lord. They made an announcement that president Trump and the first Lady have coronavirus and the debate is going on now. Trump said that he would go into quarantine. I am sure they will come up with a plan as to how /to continue the presidential debates. No matter how careful you are, you could or could not get coronavirus. Trump was sick for two days, only there is something wrong there. I don't think he had coronavirus, maybe it was a cover up because he did not want to do that particular debate. What about the first Lady; they never said anything about how she is doing? Is she alive? We will find out the truth all in good time. 21% of small businesses have closed down in Minnesota since January. Covid-19 cases grow at a speed not seen since July, the summer peak a rare complication that has been reported in kids is now showing up in adults why covid-19 is spreading again -outbreaks delay in cancer diagnosis China rapidly use of experimental covid-19 vaccines coronavirus hits beach resort, as pandemic surges in Argentina. Some Kansas city hospitals were forced to turn ambulances away as covid-19 cases jumped. Missouri,are overwhelmed by a troubling spike in covid-19 that has forced some facilities to refuse non-emergency care and others to turn away ambulances due to over occupancy.

Signs of the End Times

Average daily covid-19 hospitalizations were about 10% this week across the Kansas city region as the the midwest grapples with record breaking daily infection rates and intensive care unit beds shortages According to the mid America regional council's dashboard early this week the kansas metro area saw it's highest number of new covid-19 hospitalizations on record with the seven day average day rising to about 133 separately hospitals in the area reported 28% increase in the average number of patients on ventilators.

CHAPTER FIFTHTEEN

WAIT ON THE LORD

Slowly, little by little things will open up. At first we were going to have to wait until the end of summer for things to begin to open. Now they are doing it sooner. The restaurants and bars still have to stay closed. One restaurant owner said they were going to open up their doors anyway. Well, they will be getting a big fat fine. We must follow the rules and wait. There's that word again.

"wait" wait on the Lord. I met a man online and I can't believe we fell in love with each other. Never thought it was possible but it is. All things are possible with God. It feels like magic, it's the most beautiful feeling. He asked me if I would wait for him until he gets out of the navy; he only had a couple of months left. Then he was going to retire. I said yes I would wait for him. I have been a widow for ten years now. He has been a widower for six years. He has a twelve year old son that the nanny takes care of and his home. But it is not in the same state as me. So I asked him if he would be willing to move to my state and he said yes. That means he has to sell his house to move where I am at. Hopefully he can sell his house fast and we can find a nice home here that will suit us. I hope he and his son like Minnesota because this is where I was born and raised. This is home sweet home for me. He was supposed to come in May and we were gonna get married. Then he got transferred to South Africa to help the people there with the Coronavirus.

Signs of the End Times

Apparently it is pretty bad there. I saw on the internet that pneumonia and tuberculosis are also very bad there. When Kirik landed there and got his ipad set up he texted me. He wanted to know if I was okay then they went to some little town. He was so stressed out. He was the leader of five other guys.

Well, that was the last I heard from him. I hope he didn't get sick. I got worried then I told my daughter. She said maybe he can't get the internet where he's at. I said he got a hold of me when he first got there. My daughter said yeah but maybe the next place they sent him they had no internet access. Well that helped me to calm down quite a bit. Now I am not worried as much. I just pray for his safety. And wait, there's that word again "wait" wait on the Lord. We still are quarantined to our apartments and have our food brought to us. Like we are prisoners. They are talking about opening the dining room up again and seeing how that works. And if the numbers start going up for people getting coronavirus then we go back to being served in our apartment. I think we shouldn't try it because how are we going to sit six feet from each other in the dining room? Somebody asked if they use regular dining dishes? They said no they would probably keep using the paperware.

I guess they need all the help they can get because they seem to be short on help all the time. And we eat at all different kinds of times. Lately the food has been burnt a few times. And one time the food was so bad I had to spit it out of my mouth, it was horrible." Another few times it has been too salty. A Few other times the food had too much black pepper in it.

It was too hot to eat." Still it's a lot better with this company then the other two companies that previously owned it. For now us residents get the coronavirus test every two weeks. The employees get it done every week. When we go out of the building for a few hours when we come back we get our temperature taken. The employees get theirs taken every time they come in. They are happy to report the numbers have not gone up. The doctors are trying and scientists are trying to find out as much as they can about this new disease coronavirus. We know it does do lung damage.it causes fatigue and shortness of breath. Trouble breathing. And body aches,headache,sore throat,new loss of taste or smell. Those are in addition to the original three symptoms. And chills like the flu. New symptoms: Doctors discovered muscle or body aches, headache, congestion, or runny nose, nausea,or vomiting,Diarrhea, chills, and repeated shaking. Fever cough, shortness of breath, difficulty breathing.There are reported cases of corona patients that have skin rashes, While some children and teens in spain developed psevdo-frostbite lesions called pernio,or(chilblains) on their toes which is being called covid toes, some young covid -19 patients that were otherwise healthy are suffering strokes. While others develop blood clots. Even while on anticoagulants. Broadway actor Nick Cordero had to have a leg amputated due to clotting due to the virus. Trouble with fatigue and breathing troubles may never go away, also lung damage. For the most part it takes a few months to recover from this virus and Doctors and nurses are here to help. you are not alone. We will get through this take just one day at a time"Hurricane Delta hero" shelters more than 300 dogs in his home. Weather and climate disasters could cost 20 billion annually by 2030 As hurricane Delta hurled across the Yucatan, Ricardo was minding his animal ark.

Pimentel operates Tierra de Animales wildlife sanctuary in Cancun, currently home to around 500 livestock. House pets pack animals and reptiles-most of which are kept in spacious outdoor enclosures with some access to cover shelter.

Predictably, last week's forecasters were winds were up to 145 miles per hour, speeds too dangerous for pimentel to ignore,with over half of its animals residents exposed to the elements. The caretaker did what anyone would do. He brought more than 300 dogs into his home. This man has such a big loving heart it's too bad he couldn't have a home as big as his heart."

CHAPTER SIXTEEN

A SLOW COME BACK

25 out of 200 hundred stores will open up in the mall. Entertaining bars, restaurants will open june 1st. But you can only eat outside or take out, and you have to make reservations. No walk-ins. There is a limit of 50 customers a day. But people don't listen to the rules and that's why this pandemic is not going away. How can you blame the owners of the restaurants they need to make money to pay the bills and the employees that work for them? The social gathering is way out of control. People are not sticking to a limit and wearing face masks. Not all people, some people are following the rules. But for those breaking the rules we all suffer the consequences. The president said the churches need to be open. This is essential. Playgrounds are open at public parks. There will be white circles to help people keep their distance. In Saint Louis Park, the hardware store is creating a one way flow with arrows pointing which way customers can go.

And all employees wear masks. And customers need to wear masks. Now we are not allowed to try on clothes in any store in any dressing room. They might as well close them all down if we can't use them. If we go too fast we could get a second wave of this Coronavirus and it will hit us bigger and harder than the first wave. As the experts are saying. We must put our trust in the Lord. Whatever comes our way we are ready because we have the creator and maker on our side. He will never fail us. Even when things look really bad Casinos open up slowly. New rules,new guidelines. Nevada case count now stands at more than 9,600 and as of Sunday afternoon 438 people have died. But the case involves the woman of power. Is nowhere to be found in grim totals despite the fact she stayed tested positive. Was hospitalized and recovered in los Vegas. They opened up the dining room again, and now they are serving lunch only to see how that goes.

Breakfast and dinner is served at our apartments. If the numbers go up we will have to have all three meals served at our apartment again.

Another black man was shot in the back seven times and now is paralized for life.

And no one knows why this man was shot so many times. He was just trying to get in his car. Apparently he ran when he saw the police. Some woman called the police and said that her ex was there and that he was not supposed to be there. So the man who got shot was just trying to keep peace between them. But to no avail it did not happen. In the end the man got hurt for life for trying to help. I bet he'll never try to help a couple make peace again so sad.

Apparently they found a knife in his car on the passenger's side. They showed this man on the news he said don't take life for granted because it could be taken away in a snap of a finger just that quick he is glad to be alive. Even though he is paralized for life from the waste down. He is happy and grateful to be alive. Now what happens to the policeman that shot him seven times? Probably nothing.

It's not right"that the policeman got away with this. And why did he shoot him? There was no cause.This is really sad.

The man has six children, three were in the car with him and they saw everything happen. Apparently the man is suing the police for 10 million dollars. All the money in the world is not going to make up for the loss of use of his lower body. The coronavirus cases are now rising in almost every state in the U.S. 225,000 people have surpassed. Looks like we are going through a second wave. The difference between the one we are in now is that the covid-19 is rising everywhere on the campaign trail, President Donld Trump has taken to calling covid-19 fake news media conspiracy." But the numbers don't lie: Daily new cases are running at record levels and climbing fast. We're well into a third wave of hospitalizations,And there is worry that deaths may be rising. France and Germany thrust into lockdown as the second covid-19 wave sweeps Europe Berlin/Paris(Reverso french President Emmanuel Macron German chancellor Angela Merkel ordered their counties back into lock down. As a massive second wave of corona infections threatened to overwhelm Europe before winter. World stock markets went into a dive response. Over 3 million cases reported of coronavirus in the midEast. The lockdown for England will be extended beyond December. NYC authorities shut down a packed halloween party,indoors nearly 400 guests. Over 387 people violated coronavirus related emergency orders in attending the illegal bar/party, and nine organizers were charged with multiple misdemeanors.

Now as far as elections go a lot of people have voted already. 92 million have already been cast for the 2020 election. The race is too close between Trump and Biden In Wisconsin they will have to recount and there are six states that are undecided. Too much talk going around that some ballets have been filled out with a sharpie marker yet that will still be counted. Also talk that the ballets have been tampered with. They have to be recounted. But they have been reassured that the ballots have not been tampered with. The volunteers that have been hired to help get a background check and everything before they are hired to work this campaign. Even though Trump is acting strange he told the people to stop the voting because he won. And Biden calls Trump George.

How crazy is that?" yikes i am scared if Biden gets in office when he has dementia. This world is really crazy and getting worse everyday. The Trump campaign sues Michigan while protesters try to stop ballot count.

Tensions escalated in Detroit following a dispute over election -observer access at the city's main absentee-ballot counting center. The Trump campaign filed a lawsuit in Michigan seeking to halt the counting of absentee ballots. Less speculation, more information, opinion"Trump already won, Joe Biden makes gains in Pennsylvania, Georgia as election count continues Sean Spicer, breaking with Trump, says he sees no signs of voter fraud. The CNN's anchor said the President is like an obese turtle on his back failing in the sun, realizing his time is over. CNN"s Anderson Cooper shocked viewers on

Thursday with a particularly vicious take after President Donld Trump railed against the legitimacy of the Democratic process, spread conspiracy theories and claimed victory despite still-uncertain election results, in a remarkably dishonest speech. To the media. That is the president of the United states. The most powerful person in the world. And we see him like an obese turtle on his back failing in the sun, realizing his time is over he just can"t accept it and he wants to take everybody down with him including this country. Joe Biden our new president. The US.just set a staggering new covid-19 daily case record with more than 120,000 in infections. And it was the second day in a row the country reported more than 100,000 in infections. Health experts had warned weeks ago that the nation's daily cases would reach six digits,but those alarming figures hit sooner than expected. And covid-19 deaths could reach 266,000 by the end of November, According to an ensemble forecast published by the centers for disease control and prevention at least 121,054 new cases nationwide,According to John Hopkins University. There were at least 1,187 reported deaths, a near 20% increase from the same day last week. As the US. continues to shatter daily cases records, So do states across the nation: Colorado, Illinois Minnesota,Pennsylvania, Utah and Wisconsin are among those that set new daily records for infections. In just 10 months more than 9.6 million people in the US have been infected with coronavirus, and more than 234,000 have died. Hospitalizations are also surging nationwide. With more than 53,000 hospitalized with coronavirus as the pandemic continues to escalate,some officials are enacting some new rules to try to control the virus spread, Ohio saw a record number of new coronavirus cases infections, and it also reported it's highest number of hospitalizations and people in intensive care. The state reported 4,961 new covid-19 cases, with 2,075 people hospitalized and 571 in ICU. Every country in the state is seeing a significant community spread,who attributed the rise in cases to weddings and funerals and other social gatherings. It is everywhere we can't hide from it, we have to face it." Utah hit a daily record with 2,807 corona cases. That's up from last week when the seven day average was 1,578, according to the state epidemiologist the report was

"grim" news and it is discouraging. Gary Herbert warned that the state would only see higher numbers in the coming weeks unless residents changed their behavior.

But he added he didn't want to close businesses to curb the spread -we think that may be the wrong direction to go, Maybe some modifications of behavior that need to take place to keep those businesses open

CHAPTER SEVENTEEN
FACING THE UNKNOWN

Well my friend has been doing research on this man that I am supposed to marry. We don't get it, it's like he doesn't exist. Now he said that he was in the navy for 22 years and was going to retire. My friend looked it up and according to the records of the navy he only joined a few months ago. Now this is getting creepier by the day. He has not been active on facebook or messenger in months. It's like he disappeared. This remains a mystery. I am at a "awe wow." This world is getting more strange everyday and the people in it I don't even want to go there. So sad another young african black man has been killed for no reason. Accept racism and being prejudiced. The young black men keep getting killed. The four officers involved were fired. Apparently they were wearing cameras and they happened to be on. And a person walking by heard the young man telling the police officer that he could not breath. So the person on the street videoed on their phone what happened. Then they showed it on the news. The young man seems to have health issues. The police officer had him pinned down with his knee pressing hard in his neck. The man kept saying he couldn't breathe. but the police said to him "well get up then". The guy on the ground was calling for his mother and saying he can't breathe. People on the sidewalk said his mother is not even alive; she is dead.

The people on the sidewalk told the officer to let the man go. But he would not. In fact the police man pulled out some maze out of his pocket ready to spray somebody if they got too close. So the people watching watched the young man go limp slowly. This is inhumane injustice. Because the man wears a uniform and badge he has authority and power to do what they want if they want. They should also follow the law. They should go to prison for murder. There would be alot locked up. Sad but true. Too much hate in this world is not enough love, peace, joy, forgiveness and all the good things that the Lord gave us to use and practice. The world covers up all the good with material things, money, then let their heart get hardened, stoney. hatred, and unforgiveness. Then people try to get revenge then we get war. We always have war with somebody. Because we are not perfect. And we are bound to make mistakes. If we learn from our mistakes that is a good thing. Don't make the same mistake twice. Now there is a riot." People are holding up signs and protesting for justice for the young man that was just murdered. They did the same for Rodney King and many others. It only gets worse. Now it will be a matter of time when they kill another innocent black man because of their hatred. So sad. Nothing can be done to prevent it from happening.

That's the way of the world now. We have to face the unknown whether it's good or bad. We need to embrace ourselves for what lies ahead. There are new rules in Vegas and Hawaii and other places if you want to go to visit. Post pandemic Las Vegas Nevada case count stands at more than 9,600 and as of Sunday afternoon 438 people have died. But the case involving the woman with power is nowhere to be found. In grim totals despite the fact that she stayed tested positive, was hospitalized and recovered in Las Vegas. New rules: social distancing,reportedly drew large crowds failing to social distancing in consistent temperature checks,and general lack of safety protocols in Nevada and Clark county where Las Vegas is located. Saw record daily increases in the corona cases two weeks after opening up the gaming board has since enforced a stricter rules on cassinos, though still refusing to wear a face covering which is a requirement. Unfortunately The national scene is compounded by knucklehead behavior instances.

CHAPTER EIGHTEEN
A RIOT AND LOOTING

People are very upset about the police killing the black man. Unnecessary. People say George was a sweet kind gentleman, friendly, willing to lend a helping hand. Yet he was passing counterfeit 20 dollar bills. George kept saying he can't breathe but the officer had his knee down hard with pressure on George's neck and his nose pressed so hard against the sidewalk he nearly had his nose broken. The police held him down for 9 minutes. When George got to the hospital he died. There were four policemen there.

One of them should have had the sense enough to get the officer off George so that he could breath. Now the four officers have been fired from their job. Where is the justice? These four men committed murder. They should not get away with it. Just because they wear a uniform and badge and carry a gun doesn't give them the right to do injustice. They should follow the laws as well. This kind of treatment needs to stop toward the blacks, browns, oranges, reds, yellows, and whites. And every color in between. Change needs to happen for the good, for the people. We are supposed to feel safe and comfortable to talk to police or ask for their help. Now we have riots everywhere. There's fire everywhere. The buses stop running. The gas stations are closed in Saint Paul. Now the elderly and low income people have to suffer from these riots. Because how are they going to get around with no buses? And what are they going to do with no drugstore to get their medicine? *How* are they going to get food or toilet paper if the store is burnt down? It doesn't pay to try to get even because the innocent will be the ones getting hurt. Some of the stores will stay shut for good. What a big mess. People are pulling together to lend a helping hand. Then I heard George had a criminal record. Whatever the case, he did not deserve to die like he did. We sure do need all the help we can get. We can't forget we have a big issue called the Coronavirus to deal with as well. We will try our best to try to stay healthy.

Wearing these masks is really bothersome. It's hard to breathe with them on. Don't know if they really are helping. Sometimes when it is humid outside you feel like you are going to suffocate with the mask on. A nurse did send a list that if not used properly the mask can be very dangerous. My daughter scared me because she had the mask on while in her car on a really hot day. She said that she did not feel too well, that she felt sick and strange and that she had her mask on while in the car driving. I told her to take off the mask, that you are not supposed to wear a mask when you are in the car. I told her I sent her a list that I got from a nurse concerning the danger of wearing a mask improperly. But people went too far and said that if you wear it too long it could cause carbon dixication and oxygen efficiency. But that is not the truth, only rumors. They shut off the electricity and a young girl needed it for the ventilator to help her breath. How is she going to breathe? If I go outside I do wear a mask. I follow the rules, that's why rules are made. Now the mayor has given a curfew to all the protesters. 8:00 pm people have to be inside. They have called the national guard and they are here to help. They will shoot with flash bangs and plastic bullets which causes some pain and a little damage. One guy had to get 17 stitches on his head. They don't care if you are a good guy or not, if they see you outside they will shoot. A lot of people are coming from out of town to join in the protesting. They are taking their license plates off of their cars. One woman sits in her wheelchair and cries because she doesn't know how she will get to a grocery store or drug store. Because she lives in a highrise for low income people. And the stores were right across the street for her. Now they have been burnt down. What is she and everybody else going to do? The buses don't run. This riot is hurting the wrong people.

CHAPTER NINETEEN

BEHIND THE SCENES

This is the deadliest pandemic in history. A woman scientist stepped forward and named names about the corruption that has been going on for many years. She decided to break the silence. She even wrote a book about it. She was there when they revolutionized the virus aids. Apparently she saw it all. It's all about money. When isn't money involved? In fact these corrupt people called this woman a fugitive of justice. They put her in jail for no cause. She had 97 witnesses that could not even testify on her behalf. She said that she was unable to get a lawyer. And there's this big shot millionaire that was able to make important decisions. He had no Doctor degree, no knowledge of the medical field and no experience. Yet they let him make very important decisions. Why? Just because he had money. Now that is not right. No wonder our country is in shambles. People that run it are naive and corrupt. June 1st restaurants can open if you eat outside on the patio.

Hair salons are supposed to open as well. There are new rules to follow. We are still taking precautions. College students are filing lawsuits against the schools. The highly infectious disease has taken more than 100,000,000 lives nationwide. The government is using people. There is no vaccine that cures diseases. 3.7 million dollars flowed from the national guard of the institute, a great way to control people. So many people are caught up in fear. 13,000,000 for medicare treatment. The ventilator is the wrong treatment that is misguided. 23

hundred doctors have been treated for the Coronavirus and were given the medication. But they keep the vaccine from the people.

NIAID paid millions and killed millions since 1984. Why would you close the beaches when the sand and the ocean have sequences, healing soil micro's in the sea.? Why take something good away that is natural? and that can help us at a time of desperate need. The government said that we could go out more but with precaution. The numbers started to go up again concerning the coronavirus. We need to go forward and not backwards.

We are taking it slow. Is this virus ever going to go away for good? I sure hope so.

CHAPTER TWENTY
THERE'S A BRIGHTER TOMORROW

We did get a late Christmas gift We did get a corona vaccine in January. Most of us had no side effects, but our arm hurt real bad," to be able to move it for a couple of days. We will get the second vaccine in February. It is said that another vaccine is being developed to be better than the first where you only need to take one shot."But we will see what they come up with as long as it works and it's not endangering our well being. I will go for it." In the meantime we wait to see how this new drug is going to help if it's going to help. And if not, we will keep trying to get the right formula and dose to make the right vaccine that will work."Because we have all the time we need to succeed indeed." Secretary of defense Mark Esaper said that he does not support using active duty troops to quell the large scale of protest across the united states triggered by the death of George Floyd.

Those forces should only be used in a law enforcement role as a last resort. Comments that came after President Donald Trump recently threatened to deploy the military to enforce order. Esper's attempt to distance himself from Trump's view on using the military to restore order went over poorly. At the White House, where he was already viewed to be on shaky ground, multiple people familiar with the matter said the national guard began using tear gas as well as plastic bullets. They have become more aggressive. Now when the Governor gave a curfew he pleaded with the people and said please stay in your home by 8:00 pm because they can't tell the good people from the bad people. That they were going to shoot. All across the country and in different cities they are protesting for what happened to George Flyod. His family deserves justice. And this is what the people are saying. But they are going about it in the wrong way. It's God's battle not ours; the battle belongs to the Lord. There will be a breakthrough for justice for George. Maybe not in this lifetime, but the lifetime to come. And there will be a cure for the Coronavirus soon. Then no more people will have to die from this horrible disease. Twelve young adults went out to a nightclub, they didn't take precautions, they did not wear masks nor did they follow any of the guidelines of keeping safe. All twelve of them got the Coronavirus. They all had different symptoms. Apparently they got the virus mildly, Which they were fortunate. Now they announced that the Grand Casino is opening up. We will see what happens if people take precaution or let their guard down. The police shot another black man in the back as he was running. He was a husband and a father. A few days later they find two black men hanging from a tree. They say it was suicide. I know that those were not suicide but I can't prove it. Now the grass growing around the tree where the man was hung is buried with candles, balloons, flowers, and photographs one with him in his cap and gown and another with his sisters. A giant American flag flies over head as people gather around the tree absorbed in despair for another black life lost. Juneteenth celebrations nationwide protest against racism. And police brutality gives new urgency to a holiday long cherished by African Americans. There is this nursing home where all the people were dying everyday. The employees were scared to go to work. But there was this one woman that stayed determined to save the lives of the people that lived there.

This woman went downstairs in the refrigerator and found a bunch of dead bodies that were the residents. They ran out of bags to put the people in so they started piling the dead bodies, on top of each other.

Signs of the End Times

This Coronavirus was hitting this nursing home badly. When you went into the building it stunk like death. So they decided not to let anybody come into the building. Then a man came up with a cure that kills the Coronavirus with air purifying bags. You put them in your house and it cleans the air. They put them in the nursing home and the old folks started to feel better they could breathe better. They were not coughing as much. They had more energy and they felt younger. They wanted to get up and boogie-dance. Soon they will be available for the public to buy. The bag is called breath green. I also saw a woman demonstaight a plugin that is supposed to clean the air for viruses. Help is on the way. The police are working on the new laws of change. We are getting cure's for this deadly disease. Change is coming! I believe there's a brighter tomorrow.

CHAPTER TWENTY ONE

NEVER ENDING STORY

Well everything opened up across the United states. In Texas the Coronavirus peeked up real high again so they had to close the bars and restaurants again. In Minnesota, they peeked up also. They call it "covid Hell" As the experts say we haven't seen anything yet. That the worst is to come. As the coronavirus explodes now they are catching policemen mistreating their authority. At the beach a white woman called a black woman a nigger" so the black woman punched her in the face. I guess the white lady asked for it. There is a black man that is walking from Tennessee to Minnesota for George Fylod. How sweet that is of that man. I sure hope nothing bad happens to him because Minnesota is not a good place to be right now if you are black. Minneapolis city council votes to replace the police department with a new organization.

Police departments need better training to handle mental health emergencies. Experts. Police apologize for the behavior at the protest and declare an end to the use of tear gas. After a woman dies from breathing complications from tear gas. Officer charged with strangulation after being caught on camera. Well now the drug company wants to charge thousands for Coronavirus treatment.

Who's to say it will work? Key points: The Coronavirus is spreading rapidly and broadly for the U.S. to get it under control and prevention as some other countries have. And in Minnesota There were nearly 4,000 new infections making it the third day in a row the state broke a daily high of new cases. The State's health department also reported the days in a row where there were more than 100 new people hospitalized with coronavirus. (Battle over a shut down) rampantly in El paso county that a fourth mobile morgue was headed to the area this week.

County Judge Ricardo Samaniego, the top Government official in the country, ordered a two week shutdown of all non essential services last week. Without such measures, we will see unprecedented levels of deaths.

But the Texas attorney general said his office has filed a motion for temporary injunction to stop the judge's unlawful lockdown order, filed in the face of the Gov. Gregg Abbot's executive orders on covid-19" Abbot's said Samanie went illegal " shut down businesses. He said the county judge made it clear that he had not been enforcing existing protocols allowed under law"that could help curb the virus while following businesses to safely open from curfews to mask candidates. To crowd control, other state and local officials are screaming to control covid-19 during what Doctors will say will be the worst surge yet. Hospitals are running out of Doctors, nurses and beds for the people. They are canceling surgeries to make room for covid-19 The Morgue is full. Massachusetts Gov. Charlie Baker announced a stay at home advisory earlier this week. That will be going into effect from 10:pm to 5:am daily. Baker also announced new restrictions around gatherings, and new closing times for indoor facilities,theaters and other venues. Connecticut announced new capacity limits on restaurants, religious ceremonies and indoor event spaces. Gov. Ned Lamont also recommended residents stay home between 10pm to 5am to limit the spread through social gatherings. A primary source of infection during this fall surge. Those who can not work from home may be at higher risk of getting covid-19.

Employed adults who tested positive for covid-19 more almost twice than those tested negative, were more likely to report regularly going to a workplace than those who tested negative, according to research published centered for disease control and prevention Morbidity and Mortality weekly report. ACDC-led team looked at 314 US adults: 153

were symptomatic and had positive covid-19 pcr tests and 161 were symptomatic people with negative results, of 248 participants who reported their tele work status in the two weeks before the illness on set those who had positive covid-19 test results. Results are more likely to report going exclusively to a workplace. Florida reports 6,820 new confirmed cases, the most in almost 3 months. US becomes first nation to cross 10 million covid-19 cases as third wave in infections surge. President elect Joe Biden promises to roll out covid-19 task force on Monday. I don't think man has an answer to this never ending story,in the end the righteous and the strong will survive.

Romans: 2-2:b5 And we boast in the glory of God not only so. We also glory in our sufferings,because we know that suffering produces perseverance, character, hope and hope does not put us to shame. Because God's love has been poured out into our hearts through the holy spirit who has been given to us.

CHAPTER TWENTY TWO

GOING IN CIRCLES

Michigan and Washington on Sunday joined several other states in announcing renewed efforts to combat the coronavirus as more than 11 million cases of covid-19 have been reported in the United States with the most recent million coming in less than a week as many as americans prepare to observe aThanksgiving holiday marked by the pandemic. Michigan Gov. Gretchen Whitmer's adminastration

Ordered high schools and colleges to stop in person classes. Closed restaurants to indoor dining and suspended organized sports.

Including the football play off in an attempt to curb the states' spiking case numbers. The order also restricts indoor and outdoor residential gatherings, closes some entertainment facilities and bans gyms from hosting group exercise classes. New rules are set to last three weeks, are extensive but not sweeping the Democraric Governors stay at home order this past spring. When she faced criticism from a republican led legislature that refused to extend the state's coronavirus emergency of decoration and authorized a lawsuit challenging Whitmer's authority, to combat the pandemic she faced push back from those who opposed the decision to toughen rather than to relax. The situation has never been more dire. Whitmer who authorities say was a target for a kidnapping plot. Spurred on by anger. Over the earlier virus measures. Said at a sunday news conference." We are at the recipe and we need to take action." The directives come from Michigan the same day. That Governor. Lay Insee announced the state wouldn't force new restrictions on businesses and social gatherings. For the next month as it, too continue to combat a rising number of cases Tuesday gym and some entertainment indoor services retail stores,including grocery stores, will be limited indoor capacity and multiple household, indoor or social gatherings will be prohibited unless attendees have quarantined 14 days or tested negative for covid-19 and quarantined for a week. By Wednesday restaurants and bars will be limited to outdoor dining and orders to go. Here we go again in circles, having been through this already. We need to go forward, not in circles. Bars will be limited,again. Actions also follow grim milestones passed by Texas and Caloronia last week as each state marked more than one million confirmed covid-19 since the beginning of the pandemic. In Texas sporting events were cancelled at least one city added mobile." Mobile morgues in anticipation of hospitals, of overwhelming virus deaths. Meanwhile

California is the nation's most populous state and the first one to order a stay at home order." Officials urged those plans. Doctors fear more deaths as Dakoda experiences virus sorrow." Texas cost surpassed 20,000 confirmed coronavirus deaths on monday. As covid-19 virus continues to surge in the United States.

That is the second -highest death count over all in the U.S. Trailing only New York,according to researchers from John Hopkins University. It's the 22nd highest per capita at 69.7 deaths per 100,000 people so far, Texas leaders have given no indication of forthcoming restrictions from gathering, and spreading the virus. Instead republcian Gov. Gregg Abbott in days has been emphasizing that the new therapeutics and vaccines are expected to become available soon. A state appeals court last week sided with Texas Attorney General Ken Paxton and lifted a local shutdown order in El Paso, where mobile morgues are being trucked into helping overwhelmed hospitals and funeral homes. The Elpaso county morgue reached out to the Elpaso sheriff's department public affairs for help. After it became overwhelmed." Director Chris A Costa, inmates of the county detention faculty's trustees were asked to help for

Signs of the End Times

2 dollars an hour. Acosta said in a statement that between four and eight participants of the detention facility's trusty program have volunteered since November 9th They are accompanied by a sheriff deputy and two detention officers. The officers are equipped with personal pertective gear. The volenteers are minimum custody inmates, with misdemeanor offenses, A costa is waiting for the national guard to take over. Texas is also America's first state to record more than one million confirmed covid-19 cases last week; it also recently surpassed California the most populous state in the highest number of positive tests in the coronavirus test. The true number of infections is higher because not everyone has been tested. And studies suggest that people can be infected and not feel sick. Cars line up for the corona test at the University of Texas Elpaso During the summer people with covid-19 overwhelmed hospitals in Huston and in Rio

Grande"a valley along the border with Mexico. But in the fall case numbers dipped. And Abbott began relaxing. Some coronavirus restrictions, allowing more people in the restaurants and gyms he also let county leaders decide if they want to open up bars at 50% capacity. Since then the virus has spread. Over the past two weeks the virus has spread daily; new cases have increased by 3,430.4, an increase of 53.6% Texas now ranks 31 in the country for new cases per capita, with 428.3 new cases per 100,000 people over the past two weeks. One in every 417 people in Texas tested positive in the past week. Meanwhile, the U.S. supreme court said that the Texas department of criminal justice had substantially met the demands of the inmates at a Houston area facility for safety equipment. The courts agreed with a federal appeals court, which previously cancelled a federal appeals court, agreed with a federal appeal for federal judges for April's order for TDCJ to provide the inmates with hand sanitizer, masks, and unrestricted access to soap.

Justices Sonia Soto mayor and Elena Kagan dissent. As U.S. coronavirus cases soar 200,000 a day holiday travel is surging, total coronavirus in the United States have topped 12 million, cases are approaching 200,000 in a day,as health experts warn a new alarming new stage in the pandemic's spread while americans embark holiday travel, that could seed more outbreaks. A fall wave of the virus ushered in by colder weather is only worsening, out pacing expansions, testing and making nationwide records routine. The country passed 11 million just a week ago, And a daily infections are on track to double since Nov.4th

CHAPTER TWENTY THREE

MOVING FORWARD

The world is still in the early stages of the effort of protecting people against covid-19. Even after vaccines are approved by regulators, drug makers and public health officials still face the task of producing billions of doses and administering them to people around the world. Pollard, an ametaur mountaineer, compared the work in the task to climbing a mountain. I think we're still at the bottom of the mountain in some ways we've done the route into the bottom of the mountain. The long trek to get to the start. Now we've got to get the data of the vaccines. And then we got that huge effort to climb up to the top where we got a vast majority of those who are at risk vaccinated. Two other drug markers,Pfizer and Moderoa, this week reported preliminary results from late -stage trials showing that their covid-19 vaccines were almost 95% effective. Pollard said there is no competition between the vaccines although it will take a few to figure out the right one to use,we are in the testing phase in December. We hope to have a vaccine ready for the public. I guess you could say it would be considered a Christmas gift. What a wonderful gift to be rid of this evil disease that took a lot from us. And still is. I feel sad for the people that work the front lines, they put their life and their families lives at risk everyday. There is a Doctor who's parent's where in the nursing home and the nursing home got hit hard with the virus both of this Doctors parents died from the coronavirus and everyday this man goes to help people in the pandemic in the front line, I know he feels like crying sometimes because he is reminded that his parents died from the covid -19 and that he misses his parents. But now there is hope, there is faith, there is a cure In christ Jesus' ' So let us move forward with joy, peace, love. What about your friends, family, neighbors? Experts who offered back tactics to help encourage others to adopt a behavior shown to help stop the spread of covid-19 which has killed more than a quarter million americans. Earlier in the pandemic, the message on masking was mixed, but months later Doctors, healthcare workers, scientists and government officials are strongly encouraging people to cover their face when they are around other people along with frequent hand through hand washing, avoiding others when they are sick. And social distancing. Wearing a mask reduces droplets, spray could save lives. And here's how to put more masks on more faces, and find common ground.

CHAPTER TWENTYFOUR

WORKING THE FRONT LINES

Nurses, doctors use social media to plead for the public to take covid-19 seriously and follow safety guidelines." We are physically, socially and mentally exhausted." I have seen so many emergent intubations, I've seen more people sick than I've ever seen in my whole life." Dr. Kate Grossman said. Lacie, a nurse from the ICU, said she just got done working her third twelve hour shift this week. That she has marks on her face from the equipment she has to wear, that they are understaffed and that the people are not getting what they need. That they have ten units for covid cases and one is for the patient to go there and die. She described a sense of frustration and experation at the disconnect between what she and her colleagues did to save lives in the hospital. And what some people are doing to flaunt safety guidelines outside the hospital. We're tired, we're understaffed, we're taking care of very very sick patients, and our patient load just keeps going up. We're exhausted and frustrated that people aren't listening to us.`` Gooch said she has patients that don't believe in the covid-19 even as they are hospitalised for it. Oh boy!" it kind of blows my mind" and it is fustrateing." Gooch recalled driving to the hospital one night for an overnight shift and passing a car festival that was packed with people, most not wearing masks. I was just shocked,"and it was infuriating." she said,it just kind of feels like a slap in the face" to all the hard work that we are doing."Nine months into the coronavirus pandemic the united states remains the most affected nation with about 12 million diagnosis cases, covid-19, but not all state and local governments nor private businesses follow those guidelines. Nurses and nurses practitioners, physician assistants, and doctors and therapist who are in the hospital we see it. And it is so disheartening and demoralizing to leave work and just not see it.

To see people gathering talking about their thanksgiving plans, and their traveling plans. To see people waiting outside in a line of a bar waiting to get inside. When you're driving home from work after a horrible day. It's upsetting that more Americans than ever are hospitalised with covid-19 ahead of thanksgiving. 83,870 were hospitalised in the U.S. on Sunday, of coronavirus, while 921 people died and millions have been screened at the airports. Health care workers urge Americans to scale back Thanksgiving, more people are hospitalised than ever before, as cases continue to rise deeply amid the countdown to a thanksgiving holiday many fear will have disastrous effects, given mass travel and indoor gatherings. According to Johns Hopkins University, the U.S. has now recorded 12,248,118 cases; there were 142,732 new positives on Sunday down from the record high on Friday,when more than 196,000 cases were recorded. But 83,870 people were hospitalized. 921 people died. The death toll was 256,589 on friday,1,448 people died- the equivalent of one death every minute. The doctor saw how stressed I was so she came over to me and started to pray for me, which felt like a piece of covering fell upon me that felt so peaceful and safe and calm, I wish I could feel that way all the time. The Doctor said loud and clear to Heavenly Father,I pray that you will protect my sister Barbra,she is a lab technician in Bel Air MD she is essential during these times as she courageously serves to help treat research for all patients in need and especially those who may be suffering from the covid-19 virus. She says she's battling the most challenging time of her career and life. Doing covid testing and caring for patients on so many levels, please pray as she also battling issues with her stomach and seeing a GI Doctor. She is definitely essential to me, so as we trust in him and live without fear, I pray that he will provide mercy and love and keep her safe. In Jesus' holy name Amen.

Donld Trump faced criticism for a lack of action. The one lame duck president played golf on Sunday.

CHAPTER TWENTY FIVE

HOW TO TALK TO OTHERS ABOUT COVID MASKS

Many of us have probably seen someone in passing who wasn't wearing a mask. But you didn't stop that person and ask them why," Experts who offered science-backed tactics, to help encourage others to adopt behaviour known to help stop the spread of covid-19. Which has killed a quarter million Americans, earlier in the pandemic the messaging was mixed, but months later Doctors, health care workers, scientists, and government officials are strongly encouraging people to cover their face when around other people.

Along with frequent hand washing. Avoiding others when you are sick. And social distancing. Wearing a mask reduces droplet spray and could save lives. Your mask helps protect those around you. Your mask offers some protection to you too.

And here's how to get more masks on more faces. Find a common ground. While some Americans might downplay the pandemic, we all had shared experiences shaped by this new reality. When starting a conversation with somebody that is skeptical of the latest science and public health guidelines, try to find common ground. It's understandable to feel fatigue of the pandemic, connecting that to a preventable measure. And then start the conversation" it's all about normalizing the experience and anchoring people to resist adopting new behaviors. However, there are some do's and don'ts about wearing a mask. A mask is not a substitute for social distancing. Masks do not have to be worn if you are outside by yourself. CDC is still studying the effectiveness of the different types of masks. We will update our recommendations as new scientific evidence becomes available.

CDC does not recommend that when you wear a face shield that you don't want to wear without a mask, They recommend wearing a mask with the shield. And when you purchase a mask it should have two layers of cloth, also be sure you wear the mask right i've

Seen people wearing them wrong they might as well not wear anything, they did not have their nose or mouth covered, please wear it properly. Then it will be effective for everyone.And it would have served its purpose. In keeping everyone safe. After all that's the purpose of you wearing it right. Wear a mask that covers your nose and mouth securely under your chin, masks should be worn by people two years or older, masks should not be worn by children under two. For people who have trouble breathing, experts didn't know the extent to which people with covid-19 could spread the virus before symptoms appeared. Nor was it known that some people have covid-19 but don't have any symptoms. Both groups can unknowingly spread the virus to others. These discoveries led public health groups to an -about face on face mask. The world health organization and the U.S. centers for disease control prevention(CDC) now include face masks in their recommendations for slowing the spread of the virus. The CDC recommends cloth face masks for the public and not the surgical and N95 masks needed by health care providers. A loose- fitting also called a medical mask, a surgical mask that protects the wearer's

-nose and mouth,

Mask safety and effectiveness cloth masks are effective, they create a barrier between your mouth and nose and those around you. This makes it more difficult for the droplets that spread coronavirus through coughs, sneezes and talking to each other. Cloth masks mainly keep you from unknowingly spreading the disease to others, but some studies indicate that they may help you from large droplets and serve as an indirect reminder to avoid touching your face. This is why wearing a cloth mask inside all retail stores and public transportation has been mandatory in Maryland science April 2020. And as more services such as getting a haircut or eating in a restaurant are being allowed, it is as important as ever to continue to wear a mask. We're all in this together.

CHAPTER TWENTY SIX
LONG-SHORT TERM EFFECTS FROM CORONAVIRUS

CDC is actively working to learn more about the whole range of short- long term health effects as socialated with covid-19. As the pandemic unfolds, we are learning that many organs are affected besides the lungs are affected by covid-19 recover and return to normal health, some patients have symptoms that last for weeks or even months after recovery from acute illness can experience persistent or late symptoms multi-year studies are underway to further investigate. CDC continues to work to identify how common these sympotns are. Who is most likely to get them, and whether these symptoms eventually resolve. The most commonly reported long-term symptoms include: Fatigue, shortness of breath, cough, joint pain, chest pain Other reported long-term symptoms include:Difficulty with thinking and concentration, sometimes memory problems (referred as brain fog) muscle pain, headache, intermittent. Fever, fst-beating or pounding heart also known as (heart palpitations) more serious long term complacations appear to be less common but have been reported these have been noted to affect differences in the system in the body,these include: cardiovascular: inflammation of the heart muscle. Respiratory:lung function abnormalitiesRenal: acute kidney injury Dermatologic: rash, hair loss

Neurological: smell and taste problems, sleep issues, Psychiatric: depression, anxiety, changes in mood. The long-term significance Of these effects is not yet known. CDC will continue active investigation and provide updates as new data emerge which can inform covid-19 clinic care as well as the public health response to covid-19.

CHAPTER TWENTY SEVEN

TRUMP ON HIS WAY OUT OF THE WHITE HOUSE

Trump sitting at his desk did talk about the deadly riot at the U.S. capitol. He said I want to be very clear that I unequivocally condemn violence he said violence and vandalism have absolutely no place in our country and no place in our movement. Making America great again has always been about defending the rule of law. Mob violence goes against everything he believes in, adding, no true supporters of mine Could ever endorse political violence.

Those who engaged in the attacks will be brought to justice."He has been briefed by U.S. secret service potential threats still being planned. There must not be no violence, law breaking, and no vandalism of any kind, he said. He asked people to think of ways to ease tempers and promote peace. We will get through this challenge just like we always do,"He said.

Trump is on his way out of the white house but not out of our lives. Trump will be leaving office as a certified loser. Americans see him as subpar-president, quite an accomplishment for someone who won 74 million votes, a record foran incumbent seeking a second term.

In his own words the president's attacks on the courts. Donld Trump has displayed a troubling pattern of attacking Judges and the court for rulings he disagrees with. A pattern that began in his presidential campaign(and even before) and has continued into his presidency. This threatens our entire system of government. The courts are bulwarks of our constitution and laws, and they depend on the public to respect their judgements and on officials to obey and enforce decision Fear of personal attacks,

Public backlash, or enforcement failures should not color Judicial decision-making, and public officials have the responseablity to respect courts and Judicial decisions. Separation of powers is not a threat to democracy," Example of Trump's public statements attacking individual Judges and questioning the constitutional authority of the Judiciary, including his statements on twitter. February 24 Trump targeted U.S. Supreme Court Justices Sonia Sotomayor and Ruth Bader Ginsburg, demanding that the two Justices should excuse themselves from any cases he is involved in.

CHAPTER TWENTY EIGHT

A RIOT AT THE CAPITOL

" Trump's supporters create a riot" And it's not very pleasant to see or hear. There is confusion, there is screaming, chaos" there are gunshots being fired. There is glass being smashed in and broken all over the place. You didn't know if you were coming or going. It was scary.

U.S. capitol secured hours after pro-Trump rioters invade congress. Protesters supporting

Trump stormed in the U.S. capitol causing congress to suspend proceedings to conform the election of Joe Biden as president.

Protesters freely roamed through the capital complex, including the senate chamber, where one woman stood on the president's senate's chair and shouted Trump won state election vice president Mike Pence,who had been residing over the count of electoral college votes, was rushed out of the senate as the complex went into lockdown. As Trump's supporters began breaking and busting everything up in the complex. Several law enforcement officials said a woman who was shot by police inside the capitol building during the chaos had died. A video circulating on social media showed a woman falling from a window of a doorway in Apparently after being shot. Three other people died from medical emergencies that arose during the riot. Vice president Mike Pence was rushed out of the senate as the capitol complex went into lock down. When Trump's supporters began pouring into the building. Pence house speaker Nancy Pelosi, D Calf, and Sen. Charles

Grassley, R-Iowa, who are all in the line of presidential succession, were taken to secure locations. Members of the congress were ordered to take shelter in the complex, where at least one improvised explosive device was found. Another pipe Bomb-like was found at the headquarters of the Republican National Committee. Mark Meadows: We also know in January, but also throughout the summer that the president was very vocal in making sure we had plenty of National guard, plenty of additional support because he supports our rule of law and supports our law enforcement and offered additional help. Even in January. That was given as many as 10,000 national guard troops were told to be on the ready by the secretary of defense. Here is what we see, all kinds of blames going around" but yet not a whole lot of accountability. That accountability needs to rest with where it ultimately should be and that's on Capitol hill." Trump is the only president in U.S. history, That has been impeached not once but twice."

CHAPTER TWENTY NINE

TIME TO CLEAN UP AND CLEAR OUT

" A growing number of lawmakers are calling on president Trump to either resign or be removed. From the office following a deadly assault on the U.S. Capitol by his supporters.

After a mob stormed in the capitol forcing the building into a lockdown. Vice president Mike Pence declared Biden the winner at 3:39 am Trump said there would be an orderly transition on January 20th the closest he has come to conceding. He posted a video on twitter after his ban on the platform when it was lifted.

Biden addressed the nation calling the insurrectionists Domestic Terrorists. An air force veteran was shot and killed during the rioting. Three others died from medical emergencies, including Ben Philips who organized a bus of Pennsylvania Trump reporters. Biden says don't dare call them protesters, they were a riotous mob. Clean up continues after riots" A growing number of lawmakers are calling on president Trump to either resign or be removed from office.

Following a deadly assault on the U S capitol by his supporters after a mob stormed the capitol forcing it into a lock-down. Vice presedent Mike Pence declared Biden the winner at 3:39 am Trump said there will be an orderly transition on January 20th closest he's come to conceding. He posted a video on twitter after his ban on the platform was lifted.

Biden addressed the nation calling the insurrectionists domestic terrorists. Lawmakers demand answers to the question why there were an extremely high number of outside groups being let into the capitol. More arrests are made in connection with the capital attack. As lawmakers demand answers. Clean up continues in the capitol after rioters lead to damage and vandalism. A day rushed unto the after domestic terrorists rushed unto the grounds of the US capitol. And caused mayhem inside the facility, clean up efforts continued Thursday to fix broken windows,and cleaned floors, littered debris on thursday. Floors were covered with residue from fire extinguishers while some windows were boarded up after they had been smashed by a group of rioters. On Wednesday the crew put up additional fencing along the same spots where massive numbers of supporters for Trump stood just a day before. More than 150 others who were arrested in the capitol riot have now been identified by the FBI as radicalized militants without specific ties to any organization. A growing list of Trump's administration aids and officials have resigned from their posts. In the wake of a violent and deadly riot incited by Donld Trump With less than two weeks left of his presidency,and after years of Trump's coddling of fringe conspiracy groups and white supremacists, the president's response to the events was a bridge too far for a number of officials.

CHAPTER THIRTY

WHAT DOES TWITTER HAVE TO SAY

As rioters, many of them glad in hats bearing Trump's make America great again moto"rampaged, Senate staffing removed removed the electoral college ballots that had been on the floor of the senate for proceedings according to senate Jeff Merkley,four capable floor staff hadn't grab them they would have been burned by the mob" Merkerly tweeted other tweets, and broadcast showed shocking images of protesters dangling from the balcony Of the senate chamber, one woman drenched in blood on a stretcher and capitol police pointing guns on the floor of the representatives.

Members of the congress were being photographed wearing plastic breathing devices over their heads to protect themselves from tear gas. CNN broadcast an image of a protester sitting at Pelosi's desk with a handwritten note that said we will not back down" at her desk.

Hours after the riot began authorities began tossing flash bang grenades and dispersing teargas into a crowd of people in front of the capitol building. This is a coup attempt,Rep. Adam Kinzinger, an Illonois Rublican sen. Mitt Rommey of Utah blames Trump for the riot.

Capitol riot fall-out These are the rioters who stormed the nation's capital; the mob that rampaged the halls of congress included famous white supremacsts and conspiracy theorists. Our cameras captured the mayhem, confusion and chaos outside the capitol as Trump supporters dophile entered and disrupted certification of the electoral college results. There were non famous white nationalists and noted conspiracy theorists who have spread dark visions of pedophile satanists running the country. Others were anonymous people who had Journeyed from Indiana and South Carolina to heed President Trump's call and show their support. One person, a lawmaker from West Virginia, had only been elected to office since November. All of them converged on Wednesday on the grounds of U.S. capitol,where hundreds of rioters crash through barricades,climbed through windows,and walked through doors,wandering around the hallways with a sense of gleeful desecration,Because for a few breath taking hours, they believed that they had displaced the very elites they said they hated. We wanted to show these politicians that it's us in charge and not them." said a construction worker from Indianapolis,who is 4o and identified himself only as Aron. He declined to give his last name.

I'm not that dumb." he added we got the strength."

CHAPTER THIRTY ONE

TO SEE THE PERSPECTIVE OF THE OTHER SIDE

There were many reasons to be suspisious of the 2020 election results; there was no accountability for mail in ballets. You didn't need an ID for the mail in ballets, they were not verified in any way. There were numerous people that worked at the voting sites, they signed an affidavit that they witnessed illLegal activity. questionable activities discarding ballets. Restricting poll watchers hiding suite cases of ballets under a table in the state of Georgia. In the polling site. Bringing the suit cases out when everybody is gone then counting them in the middle of the night." They wouldn't let poll watchers do their job. They kept them too far away visually to see the ballets.

When they complained about it they got kicked out of the building. It took a judge to have to rule that they could go back in the building and watch from an acceptable distance. These kinds of things went on in all the battleground states. People call Trump a sore loser but he had a reason to contest the outcome. The 2016 election was stolen" Hillery is still not conceded. Trump is a man of his word. When was the last time a president did alot for the people in such a short time. Trump is the rock" Biden signed an executive order that stopped deportation of illegal imergrastions, convicted crimes such as muder, rape, car jackings,all crime. Trump was putting up a wall and Biden put a stop to it."

"Something is wrong", it seems as though, Biden is our enemy." But we still have to love him and respect him right." Biden is pro China " and Trump is for America. Trump was acquitted from the allegations.'so that is good.

CHAPTER THIRTY TWO

A TASTE OF THE ICEBERG

Severe weather is affecting more than 100 million Americans and snow is still falling in the hardest hit areas in Texas. These people have been without heat and electricity and running water for a while. While power is being restored to millions in Texas, nearly half of residents, 13 million, don't have access to clean running water. In the city of Kyle, officials said water should only be used to sustain life at this point." In Houston, America's fourth largest city, there are long lines for food, gas, and supplies.

Things are also bad in Oklahoma, where president Biden declared a state of emergency after the longest stretch of sub-zero temperatures there on record. At least 34 deaths were attributed to the storm, 20 of them were from Texas. The winter weather also created a political storm. Texas senator Ted Cruz was criticized for flying to Cancun with his family this week, while his constituents suffered in record-low temperatures. The San Antonio water system announced that it will begin providing water distribution at seven pump locations around the city. Residents will receive up to five gallons per person and are advised to boil the water they receive as a precautionary measure. San Antonio and the San Antonio bank will also provide bottled water distribution at sites around the city. San Antonio has experienced water outages due to the winter weather emergency, the San Antonio water system issued a boil water advisory for customers who still have access to water.

CHAPTER THIRTY THREE

HELP IN NEED, TRACKING THE VIRUS

Local organizations in Texas are using their resources to help residents in need. Warming stations across the state are still open and are urging residents to come in if their situation becomes dangerous. Organizations from outside the state are also sending teams to brave the storm. Mercy's chefs, a non-profit based in Mouthport Virginia, sent a team to Dallas to provide meals to those without water, gas, heat, or a way to leave their homes. This winter storm has affected so many people over such a widespread area in communities that simply aren't prepared for this kind of weather-we've never seen anything like it, Gary LeBlanc, founder of Mercy's Chefs, told CBS News we are glad Mercys chefs can respond quickly and get meals to those in need." Hospitals in Texas are losing resources and gaining patients. Chaotic scenes were playing out all over Texas hospitals faced an onslaught

Problems from the brutal storm: wintery indoor temperatures, a death of generators, acute water shortage and a spike in the Emergency Room visits by patients in desperate need of dialysis treatment and oxygen tanks. Were hauling in water on trucks in order to flush toilets," at Houston Methodist, which operates seven hospitals around the country's fourth- largest city. Water was in such short supply that health workers were using bottled water for chemotherapy treatments. The water challenges extended to about 13 million Texans who are told to boil water for their safety after

Burst pipes and broken water mains. Another winter storm brought freezing rain, snow and temperatures that were much below average, a gut punch for people who have restored stoves, barbecue grills and gasoline generators to stay warm. Days of glacial weather have left at least 38 people dead nation wide, made many roads impassable, disrupted vaccine distribution and blanketed nearly three quarters of the continental United States in snow. In Texas, hospitals such as St. David's South Austin medical center

Said they were transferring some patients to other facilities as they desperately tried to conserve resources. Parts of the ceiling collapsed at the Baylor University Medical center in Dallas after a pipe burst. Spraying water directly into the Emergency room. Some of the challenges facing the hospitals are tied to problems tied cascading through the state's beleaguered health care system since the storm grid crisis. Influx of dialysis patients, for instance, is placing stress on hospital Emergency rooms. Because many dialisis centers-which require elecritcity, heat and large amounts of filtered water to properly provide care. The centers are temporarily closed. At one of the care units in Houston's hospitals, Doctors turned an old intensive care unit into a makeshift dialysis unit transfering 42 patients out of the cramped emergency room. And in parts of east Texas. Health care workers are growing so alarmed about patients going without dialysis treatments. That they are asking local police to do a wellness check on them. This can be a death sentence for some of our patients."Jesse singh 58, said his father, 80 years old, was turned away from his regularly scheduled dialysis treatments. Because the clinic was having water issues. It's a dangerous situation. Mr. Singh said.

CHAPTER THIRTY FOUR

A TEXANS WATER CRISIS

Cracked pipes, frozen wells, offline treatment plants: Winter weather has disrupted hundreds of thousands of US vaccinations. Just as vaccine distribution was beginning to gather steam in the United States, brutal winter weather is delaying the delivery of hundreds of thousands across the country. The Centers for disease control and prevention projected widespread "delays" in vaccine shipments and deliveries because of weather affecting Fedex facility in Memphis and a UPS in Louisville, both vaccine shipping hubs. Now those projections are becoming true. Shipment delays have been reported in California, Colorado, Florida, Illinois, Nevada, New Jersey, Ohio, Utah, Washington and Orgen, among other states, forcing vaccine sites to temporarily shutter and coveted appointments to be rescheduled. In Texas where millions of people lost power during the powerful storm. A delivery of more than 400,000 first doses was delayed in anticipation of the bad weather. A portion of those shots, roughly 35,000 doses of Pfizer's vaccine, were sent to north Texas providers. But shipments will continue to depend on safety conditions. The state health services was asking providers that aren't able to store vaccines to power outages, to transfer eleswhere or administer it so it doesn't spoil.

Texan's files a lawsuit over 9000,00 dollar, the week of winter storm.

CHAPTER THIRTY FIVE
THE TEXAS TRIBUNE

You might have heard that Texas has its own power grid. Did you know not all parts of the state use it? Millions of Texans were left in the dark for days. After the winter storm triggered power outages. But people in El Paso, the upper panhandle and parts of east Texas kept their lights on- Thanks to power drawn from other parts of the country. Texas has an unusual power setup. Unlike the other states in the union, which are mostly inter connected, Texas has its own power grid. That grid operates as the electric reliability council of Texas, 90% of the state. The other 10% includes ElPaso, the upper panhandle and a chunk of east Texas. These areas for various reasons, including proximity, Instead get their electricity from other grid providers. For example the panhandle is closer to Kanas than to Dallas. The main culprit for the power outages in EROT's coverage area was failures across Texas. Natural gas operations and supply chains due to the extreme temperatures. From frozen natural gas wells to frozen wind turbines, all power sources faced difficulties during the winter storm. Texans largely rely on natural gas for power and heat generation, Especially during peak usage, experts said. On Feb 16 at least 4.5 million customers were without power. The operator of the Texas power grid is under investigation. The Novel coronavirus break has reached almost every corner of the globe and sickened thousands" and killed millions" and still today everyday people are getting the virus and people are dying everyday. Now that we started the vaccines maybe it will be less and less it probably won't ever go away for good. You don't know what the future holds.Effort to vaccinate American intensifies, nationwide, an alarming sign to public health experts say the tests daily covid-19 tests numbers are falling nation-wide.500,000 lives lost to covid-19.

CHAPTER 36

TRACKING THE VIRUS

One dose Johnson &Johnson covid-19 vaccine meets criteria as safe and effective,FDA report finds. Detailed information aJohnson&Johnson candidate vaccine for covid-19 raises no safety concerns,according to a report released from the Drug and Administration advisory committee, which will hold an all day meeting to review the data. which is likely to give the vaccine a thumbs up." Leading to expected autherization for the vaccine in adults within the next few days.

Johnson & Johnson covid-19 is about to be released to the public and there are some big changes you should know about the company. Also is studying two dose regimens,which might prove more effective or more durable,In which case people might be encouraged to get a booster shot. The vaccines and related Biological products advisory committee, or vrbpac is likely to sign off because it seems to have met all the criteria for the authorization the FDA established last year. Like the moderna and pfizer-biotech vaccines, the one from J&J underwent a large clinical trial, showing it's safety and effectiveness, and the company proved it can manufacture in a safe and consistent manner. The US sticks with two dose covid-19 vaccines,it will be up to the acting FDA commissioner to arica, authorize what could happen in a few days. The vaccine is already used in south Africa,and the company applied to the European Union by the world health organization for authorization J&J agreed to provide 100 million doses of it's vaccines in the USA by June, including 20 million by the end of march

Those doses will add to the 300 million pfizer-Biotech and Moderna each have promised to deliver to the US government by the end of July. The vaccine was shown to be 72% effective in a trial in the USA in which all etnnic, racial and age groups benefited about the same. Trials of the vaccine in other countries have shown less effectiveness. 66% in Latin America, 57% in South Africa, 28 days after the shots- probably because of variants of the virus circulating in those countries. The same variants are circulating in the USA but not in very high numbers,so the vaccine is likely to be useful here, particularly if it requires one dose. FDA prepares for variants: covid-19 vaccines, tests work well. The Novel coronavirus break has reached almost every corner of the globe.And sickened thousands, the virus was first detected in Wuhan, China after several people visited a live animal market where they were treated for pneumonia-like symptoms. A worker in a protective suit closed the seafood market in Wuhan, China, Jan.10,2020 The seafood market is linked to the outbreak of pneumonia caused by the new strain corona virus. As the effort to vaccinate Americans intensifies,daily covid test numbers are falling nationwide,an alarming sign to public health experts who say the tests are still crucial to containing the virus. Testing has been a fraught and highly politicized issue from the beginning of the pandemic, with the first test rolling out slowly,testing taking a while to ramp up and former president Trump wrongly claiming that an increase of testing was behind the world -leading level of coronavirus cases in the U.S. There have also been issues with testing access and the reliability of certain types of tests. The daily average for covid tests is now just one million a day as of mid- February roughly a million less from where the country was a month ago. According to the tracking project at Johns Hopkins University, the decline has been one of the steepest,of the pandemic. Testing numbers in recent days however have been climbing upward, but aren't near their level highest at the 2020 holiday season travel. So far this year testing hit its peak Jan.15, at

2.2 million tests as the virus raged at unprecedented levels. But from then on daily testing declined despite the emergence of new virus rages and cases recently appearing to plateau thigh levels. As top health officials have pointed out. CDC testing is down 30%. Look at our country as one big body, it is said there is a fourth surge ahead.We now have three highly effective vaccines" covid-19 will likely be with us forever. Here's how we'll live with it eventually, the virus could become a much milder illness-but for now, vaccination and surveillance are critical to end the pandemic phase. A nurse prays inside the corridors of the intensive care unit of RafiK in southernBeirut, Leb. As covid-19 continues to run its course the likeliest long term outcome is that the virus sars-cov-2 becomes endemic in Large swaths of the world, Constantly circulating Among the human population but causing fewer cases of severe disease. Eventually- years or even decades in the future- covid-19 could transition into a mild childhood illness, like the four endemic human coronaviruses that contribute to the common cold. My guess is enough people get the vaccine that will reduce the person to person transition. Says Paul Duprex, director of the University of Pittsburgh's center for vaccine research. There will be pockets of people who won't take the vaccines,there will be localized outbreaks, but it will become one of the regular coronaviruses." But this transition won't happen overnight. Experts say that stars-cov-2's exact post pandemic trajectory will depend on three major factors:1: How long humans retain immunity to the virus." 2:How quickly the virus evolves, 3: and how widely older populations become during the pandemic itself. Depending on these three factors take place. The world could be facing several years of halting pandemic transition- one marked by continued viral evolution,localized outbreaks,and possibly multiple rounds of updated vaccinaccines, people have got to realize this is not going to go away." says Roy Anderson, an infectious disease epidemiologist at Imperial college London,we're going to be able to manage it,because of modern medicine and vaccines, but it's not something that will just vanish.

CHAPTER THIRTY SEVEN

WHICH VACCINE IS RIGHT FOR YOU TO GET

Comparing covid-19 vaccine efficacy numbers can be misleading. The best covid-19 vaccine for you is still the first one you can get. There are three different vaccines that you can get now that are now being distributed across the united states, and all three are highly effective at the most important thing : preventing hospitalizations and deaths from covid-19. But some people remain worried that Johnson& Johnson is less effective at preventing disease to begin with. Detroit Mayor Mike Duggan turned down 6,200 J&J vaccines doses for his city. J&J is a very good vaccine. Moderna and Pfizer are the best." Duggan said at a news conference." And I am going to make sure that residents of the city of Detroit get the best. scientists say this is the wrong way to think about vaccines." and that judging J&J vaccine as inferior based on its lower reported effically is misleading. Such actions are especially worrying at the current stage of the pandemic.Covid-19 has killed over 500,000 Americans, and while cases seem to be declining, the virus is still spreading, new variants are gaining ground. And some parts of the country are already relaxing precautions (which health officials warn could end up prolonging the pandemic.) Turning down vaccine doses while supplies of all covid-19 vaccines are still stretched thin undermines the campaign to curb the pandemic. In clinical trials, the vaccines produced by Pfizer/Bion tech, by Moderna, and by J&J reduced the fatality rate of covid-19 by 100% compared to their placebo groups. They also kept all the recipients out of the hospital.

That means they can potentially down grade covid-19 from a public health crisis to a manageable problem. The goal of a vaccine was really to defang or tame this virus, to make it more like other respiratory virus that you deal with, so when we look at the three approved vaccines in the US, All of them extremely good at that metic," said Amesh Adalja, a Senior scholar at the John hopkins university. The vaccines do have some important differences.

The J&J is one dose while the others are two. It can be restored at refrigerator temperatures.

While the others require freezer temperatures. J&J is also less expensive, about

10$ per dose roughly half as much as the pfizer/BioTech vaccine. The Moderna vaccine costs between $25 to 37$ per dose. These factors give J&J an edge in logistics and could help get the shots to people in harder to reach places. Saad Omer, the director of yale Institute for Global Health, said it's a vaccine that can increase equity." But when J&J filed for an emergency use authorization from the food and drug administration for its covid-19 vaccine in early February, it reported that its overall efficacy in preventing covid-19 cases that produced symptoms was 66.1 percent. The Moderna vaccine and the pfizer/BionTech vaccines reported efficacy levels around 95 percent. That gap in efficacy numbers is fueling some people's perception. That the J&J vaccine isn't that good. Scientists say that these numbers cant be fairly compared to one another. The efficacy levels of the covid-19 vaccines are specific to the clinic trials that produced them, and those trials were not conducted in the same ways. In addition, health officials have been emphasizing that the most important numbers are how well the vaccine prevents hospitalizations and deaths. Consistent across the board and arguably more comparable. Even after vaccines have been distributed. Researchers are finding that covid-19 vaccines are a remarkable job at keeping people alive. That's why the recommendation remains that the best covid-19 vaccine for the vast majority of the people is the first one they can get." That's how I think of these vaccines, basically interchangeable,"Adalja said.

CHAPTER THIRTY EIGHT
A YEAR LIVING WITH CORONAVIRUS

Has a year of living with covid-19 rewired our brains? The pandemic is expected to precipitate a mental health crisis, but perhaps also a chance to approach life with new clarity shows your support for rigorous, independent Guardian journalism. When the bubonic plague spread through England in the 17th century, Sir Isaac Newton fled to Cambridge where he was studying safety for his family home in Lincolnshire. The Newtons did not live in a cramped apartment. They enjoyed a large garden with many fruit trees. In the uncertain times, but of ordinary life, his mind roamed free of routines and social distractions. And it was in his context that a single apple falling from a tree struck him more intriguing than any of the apples he had previously seen fall. Gravity was a gift of the plague. So how is this pandemic going for you? In different ways, this is a likely question we are all asking ourselves.

Whether you have experienced illness, relocated, lost a loved one or a job, got a kitten or got divorced, eaten more, spent longer showering in the morning, or reached everyday for the same clothes, it is an incapable truth that the pandemic alters us all. But how? And when will we have answers to these questions- because surely there will be a time when we can scan our personal balance sheets and see in the credit column something more than grey hairs, a thicker waist and a kitten? (Actually, the kitten is pretty rewarding.) What might be the psychological impact? Will it change us forever? of living through a pandemic? People talk about the return to normality," and I don't think that is going to happen, says Frank Snowden, a historian of pandemics at Yale, and the author of Epidemics and society: from black death to the present. Snowden has spent 40 years studying pandemics. Then last spring, just as the phone was going crazy with people wanting to know history, could shed light on covid-19 his life's work landed on his lap he caught the coronavirus. Snowden believes that the covid-19 was not a random event. All pandemics affect societies through the specific vulnerabilities people have created by their relationships with the environment, other species, and each other," he says. Each pandemic has its own properites, and this one a bit like bubonic plague- affects mental health.

Snowden sees a second pandemic coming. In the train of the covid-19 first pandemic, psychological pandemic." Aolfe oDonovan, an associate professor of psychiatry at the UCSF Weill Institute for Neurosciences in

California,who specialises in trauma, agrees. We are dealing with so many layers of uncertainty,she says truly horrible things have happened and they will happen to others and we don't know when or to whom and it is really demanding cognitively and physiologically. A new study in the Lancet medical journal published found the novel coronavirus lived in patients for more than five weeks. Some of the patients received antiviral medications but the drugs did not shorten the lifespan of the virus.

The 19 doctors who authered the study analyzed the medical records of 191 patients in China (135 from jinyintan hospital and 56 from Wuhm Pulmonary Hospital,) including the demographic, clinic, treatment and laboratory data of 137 coronavirus patients who were discharged and 54 patients who died in the hospital. They found that the virus was present in the bodies of the patients with severe disease status for 19 days, and inside of the bodies of patients with critical disease status for an average of 24 days. Overall, the virus was detected for an average of 20 days in patients who were eventually discharged from the hospital. In the respiratory tracts of patients who died. Coronavirus was detectable until death.

The shortest length of time the virus lived in the respiratory tract of a survivor was eight days.

And perhaps most shocking of all, in some cases,The virus persisted for as long as 37 days."This has important implications for both patient isolation decision making and guidance around the length of antiviral treatment," The authors of the study included. For weeks,the u.s. Centers for disease control and prevention has been otherwise exposed to self quarantine for 14 days. Does this study suggest the risk could persist longer? Well not necessarily. President Joe Biden said he will direct states, tribes, and territories to make all American adults eligible for covid-19 vaccine by May 1, In his first time addressing Thursday. The president also communicated that if everyone does their part to slow the spread and get vaccinated, there's a chance that families, friends, Neighbors could gather in small groups by the fourth of july. After this long hard year,that will make this

Independence day truly special where we not only mark our Independence as a nation. But begin to mark our Independence from this virus.I say Amen!"

CHAPTER THIRTY NINE
A TIME FOR RESTORATION

Things began to open up but things are not the same. A Lot of businesses closed their doors for good Things don't stay the same anyhow.

However, even with some government assistance,others will be working at first simply to recoup at their losses. The loosening of restrictions comes as vaccines have finally picked up speed in the european Union of which Poland is a member and the numbers of covid-19 infections and hospitalizations have plunged in Poland in recent weeks. Yet many people don't feel like they can relax yet.

What used to be normal suddenly has become something unbelievable" But India suffers from this deadly second wave, Ishaan Singh, a young couple from Punjab. She is a software engineer for IBM, and he's an expert in cyber security.

When the crisis hit, they dropped everything and moved to New Delhi with only a change of clothes and a ferice dedication to serve others.

At first they slept on the floor at the makeshift clinic where they were volunteering. In just three days, they and their team at the HemKunt foundation were able to convert what was normanaly a wedding tent into a large field hospital in the middle of a dirt field outside Delhi, where they have helped thousands of people.

We met one young woman outside the clinic who said the hospital told her she needed to find her own oxygen for her father. As volunteers loaded two canisters into her car, she told us without this clinic she wouldn't be able to keep her father alive. When people are turned away from hospitals, they step in to get the urgent,life saving care they need for free." We drove along with them as they delivered oxygen concentrators to homes all over the city. The look of relief in people's eyes when they saw them at their front doors is something the woman said she will never forget.

CHAPTER FORTY

IT'S NOT OVER YET BE ON GUARD

It's time to move on and sure we may have lost a lot but we have gained a lot in the process. We should have gotten stronger in our faith and within ourselves to have confidence and better self esteem. We should feel like overcomers in christ. Because without Christ we can do nothing. Yes maybe they closed the 24 hour perkins but they are putting something else in its place. Everyone was waiting for the countdown when the bars could be open again one man said it was like having a new year's countdown in the spring. Some bars were serving before midnight. People were so happy they were going around hugging everyone. And now it's not mandatory to have to wear a mask if you are vaccanated. But we still need to be cautious." We still need to wash our hands frequently, still do distandting, and avoid large crowds. It's not over yet." Be on guard.

More than 500,000 have died in the US one hundred thousand coronavirus deaths in the

U.S. was the low estimate. That figure, the bottom end of the Trump white House's best-picture scenario of 100,000 to

240,000deaths, was reached in may 2020. After the virus spread across the United States. The covid-19 death count matched the upper end of that figure in early November. The death toll in the U.S. has eclipsed those of every other country. Track the number of new reported deaths, each day in the country and in the hardest hit states. NBC will update the data in these charts daily. In the meantime people die every day. Some people won't take the vaccine, we can't force them. There was a man telling people that if you drink lemon juice it's just as effective as the vaccine."I guess it worked for him and his family. He was trying to persuade others to do it too and to not take the shot. Well to each their own. Hopefully in time we can get rid of this virus for good and that it will never return like other diseases have gone and never returned." It's possible For with God All things are possible."Luke 1:37

I say Amen! May the U.S. stands in stark contrast to countries like South Korea, New Zealand, and Singapore as it continues to report over 30,000,00 new infections per day. This is really the beginging of the U.S.'s recent surge in new cases. I think there was a lot of wishful thinking around the country that everything is gonna be fine. We're over this and we are not even beginning to be over this. A pandemic of a novel. The Coronavirus has now killed more than 502,000 people worldwide and over 101 million people across the globe have been diagnosed with covid-19. The virus, according to data compiled by the center for systems science and engineering at Saint John's Hopkins University, said the actual numbers are believed to be higher due to testing shortages, many unreported cases, and suspicions that some governments are hiding the scope of their nations outbreaks since the first cases were detected in China in December. The United States has become the worst affected country with more than 2.5 million cases and at least 125,928 deaths. Arizona reverses opening of bars, gym's, and movie theaters. The U.S. reports more than 38,800 new cases over 200 urged to quarantine after positive cases at Planet Fitness. New York records lower rise deaths since March. New York indoor dining now in question. This is an ever ending story. Things opened up too fast. Disneyworld reopens even as Coronavirus cases soar in Florida. The United States records over 7,000,000 new Coronavirus cases soar in Florida and across the United States recorded over in a single day.

Signs of the End Times

Walt Disney's Magic Kingdom and Animal Kingdom reopened on Saturday while Epcot and Disney's Hollywood studios will reopen July 15th. The most magical place on earth is open for business again even as Florida continues to rack up near records of new Coronavirus cases.

The state's 11,433 new covid-19 cases record will continue to surge on Friday. It's biggest daily increase since July 3rd when 11458 cases were recorded. The Florida health department reported 435 more hospitalizations- the state's largest single day. On Saturday, Florida reported an additional 421 hospitalizations as well as 10,360 new cases. U.S. tops 3 million known infections as Coronavirus surges; new covid-19 is rising. Coronavirus cases climb in the U.S. Southwest officials consider measures to restrict activities to contain spread. U.S. Coronavirus set another daily record of continued surges in southern and western states. More than 66,000 Coronavirus cases were confirmed in the U.S. Friday, the highest daily number since the pandemic began. Raising the country's total to nearly 3 1 half million according to data replied the U.S. accounts for a quarter of the 12.5 million reported globally. Now update U S hits over 7 million covid cases more than 200,000 lives lost in U S to Coronavirus. Dr. Fauci just warned the U S about scary new coronavirus symptoms that won't go away. Now we didn't need to hear about more negative news. We have enough to deal with already. California, Florida, Texas, Arizona, and Georgia, reported at or near record daily covid-19 cases in several other states including Alabama, Alaska, Idaho, Nevada, Oklahoma, South Carolina, Tennessee, and West Virginia increased by at least 20 percent over the last week. Updated : National figures of coronavirus deaths 147,381, cases

4392,073, testing data today 819,270 the virus is just just surging in America. It's making a world wide comeback. Tracking the spread with more than 150,000 deaths. The U.S. has the most Coronavirus fatalities in the world. Why Dr. Birix believes the virus is about to spike in the midwest. Europe is grappling with the threat of a second wave. The six types of covid-19. A 16,000-person study from King College London suggests that there are different versions of the disease and predicts which patients are likely to need the ventilators. Mounting evidence indicates that the virus spreads through air.

Scientists worry that the health guidelines are lagging. Loss of taste covid toes, what we know about the odd growing list of symptoms. This is the latest update to this never ending story.

Number of covid -19 cases in the U.S. reaches 7 million according to tales from Reuters, and the New York Times. President Trump signs executive orders aiming to extend unemployment benefits and evictions protections after stimulus talks stall in Congress amid covid-19 pandemic. The mid American conference cancelled it's fall football season, making it the first football bowl subdivision conference in the N C C A A to do so. A pill that may lesson covid -related lunge damage. Miami will be the first to test it. Next update I share of this never ending story. About the coronavirus or covid 19 Compounds the risk of faminc and food insecurity in Congo, Yemen, Northeast Nigeria and South Sudan, the UN says.

Governors of Georgia, New Jersey, and Washington to exercise caution and help the spread of covid 19 over the labor day weekend. A record of 52% of young american adults are living with their parents amid the economic downturn triggered by the pandemic, according to a Pew Research center report. Experts project Autumn surge in coronavirus cases. With a peek after election day. The way people are getting together is changing and as all continue to adjust it's important to remember that everyone is expercering the pandemic differently. As we continue to navigate this new normal, we still need to adapt our party behavior to respect other people's health and safety.

Barbecue is the star of the show. Barbecues are a classic Labor Day weekend. Activity so maybe you don't have the blow out bash of the past, but it's possible to host or attend socially distant gatherings for a few friends outdoors is the best since experts say that lowers the chance of transmission of covid 19 and there are plenty of ways to make summer cookouts less of a risk.

Including limiting shared items such as serving utensils having hand sanitizer available and restricting inside entertaining. Create an atmosphere that helps people connect in a special way. Festivities, celebrating almost always involve food. And great food is what brings good friends and family together. especially During the unusual times we are experiencing now. Such as Coronavirus,3 people die from covid 19 they were celebrating a wedding. Hurricane Laura death toll 25 in Louisiana and Typhoon in southern Japan. wildfire ln national forest. dozens of people being rescued. Hurricane Sally hit the Florida and Alabama area. One person died and over 300 hundred people were rescued.

Hurricane Teddy is following Hurricane Sally at winds at 130 miles per hour custing" They think Teddy may hit main the northern coast. But Teddy landed in the South southwestern dangerous waves and high winds. South western newfoundland. Very large swells produced by teddy and tropical storms remain flooded in effect.storms. Portions of Bermuda,the Leeward Islands,the greater antilles the Bahamas the east coast of the United States.Here's what category 4 Hurricane could look like at landfall.

Hurricane Dorian is a category 3 storm of 115 mph. But the forecast indecates Dorian may be a category 4 hurricane with winds from 130 to156 mph. When it strikes here's why it matters: meteorologists use the saffir simpson hurricane wind scale to measure hurricane's strength. The system divides storms into five categories.

Category 1:74 to 95 mph.(minor damage) category 2:96 to110 mph. (Extensive damage- can uproot trees and break windows) category 3: winds 111 to 129 mph.(Devastating can break windows and doors) category 4:winds 130 to 155 mph. (catastrophic damage- can rip off roofs) category 5: winds 157 mph or higher(The absolute worst and can level houses and destroy buildings.)

Tornadoes in Connecticut and Maryland. Gamma lashes Mexico with damaging winds and flooding rains. What about the land hurricane that nobody expected. Called the derecho. Winds of up to 1000,00 It caught farmers on fields, bicyclists on trails and travelers on highways. Unaware that a series of thunderstorms had formed the night before inSouth Dokota had picked up strength as it moved across

Nebraska at least three people in Iwa and one in Indiana were killed. Including a bicyclist on a trail and a woman sitting on her porch. Both struck by trees. Forecasters had predicted thunderstorms and in some communities tornadoes, sirens sounded 20 to 30 minutes before the winds began. But for many people there was no sense that the day would be different from any other muggy Monday in August. A farmer was driving to his parents farm a few miles away when winds of blinding rain and a wall of wind nearly pushed his pick up off the road. His corn crop was damaged, he lost two 8000,00 bushel corn bins. And seven hog buildings. His 800 animals are staying at his sister's farm. Another man was taking a nap in his home in Cedar Rapids, when the wind began to blow he said he didn't hear any sirens and that he didn't have time to get to the basement so he took cover in a closet. He was scared that he was going to die alone. The man said he wished that they would give better warning. Scientists say it's difficult to give advance warning about a derecho, because unlike more distant hurricanes forming over the ocean it's formacation is not readily apparent.

Scientists now believe that the derecho traveled a thousand miles (1,610 kilometers) from South Dakoda to Northwest Ohio.

One half of the world is drowning, the other half is burning, what happens if you bring them together, what a big mess!"New York City restaurants resume"indoor dining with 25% capacity, among other restrictions, the Governor. announced. Marriott will lay off hundreds of employees at it's Maryland headquarters because of the pandemic impact on the travel industry. Los Angeles county bans trick or treating. And cancels halloween events due to covid 19 -concerns. This is the word I received from the Lord. Letting your heart change is not harmful, change is beneficial, resisting change and resisting what I am bringing about only brings you in the only lands you are stuck in and that is where I am working on getting you out of this day. Realize there are people and situations that must be relinquished if you are to have everything that you cry out to me for. Abraham had to let go of a lot, Abigail had to let go of Nabal, the Israelites had to lose their appetites for the leeks and garlics of goshen. To see captivity broken. These are the attachments and appetites I am dealing with in your life. To be you to the place of promises fulfilled and highest hearts desires realized, be willing to sacrifice your comfort level and familiarity to move into the assignment I have set before you. I haven't called you to sit in stagnation doing nothing like all the others do nothing people around you your life counts for something in the eternities when i formed and fashioned you I folded into your character a drive and a desire to make a difference says God. Not just be different, come away from all the navel-gazers and narcissistic personalities around you. Humility is the only path that leads to which I have ordained. Let patience be replaced by anger, let frustration by a healthy dose of self-realization of just how petty the flesh is and what the enemy of faith has become. The hour is late and the door of opportunity stands open. Move forward in faith believing and refuse to look back but only ahead to that shining destiny that awaits God in truth. Now it's verses like Romans 5:2b-5 that give me comfort and hope and to keep looking to the Lord and not giving up because the Lord doesn't give up on us.

Here are five things you need to know about the Delta variant:

1. Delta is more contagious than the other virus strain.

One thing that is unique about Delta is how quickly it is spreading, says F. Perry Wilson, MD, a Yale Medicine epidemiologist. Around the world, he says, "Delta will certainly accelerate the pandemic." The first Delta case was identified in December 2020, and the variant soon became the predominant strain of the virus in both India and then Great Britain. By the end of July, Delta was the cause of more than 80% of new U.S. COVID-19 cases, according to CDC estimates. A July CDC report on Delta's transmissibility came after an outbreak that occurred in Provincetown, Mass., after a crowded July 4 weekend, which quickly turned into a cluster of at least 470 cases. While the number of reported "breakthrough" cases in general has been very low in the U.S., three quarters of those infected in Provincetown were people who had been immunized. According to the CDC, even people with breakthrough cases carry tremendous amounts of virus in their nose and throat, and, according to preliminary reports, can spread the virus to others whether or not they have symptoms. The CDC has labeled Delta "a variant of concern," using a designation also given to the Alpha strain that first appeared in Great Britain, the Beta strain that first surfaced in South Africa, and the Gamma strain identified in Brazil. (The new naming conventions for the variants were established by the World Health Organization [WHO] as an alternative to numerical names.) "It's actually quite dramatic how the growth rate will change," says Dr. Wilson, commenting on Delta's spread in the U.S. in June. Delta was spreading 50% faster than Alpha, which was 50% more contagious than the original strain of SARS-CoV-2, he says. "In a completely unmitigated environment—where no one is vaccinated or wearing masks—it's estimated that the average person infected with the original coronavirus strain will infect 2.5 other people," Dr. Wilson says. "In the same environment, Delta would spread from one person to maybe 3.5 or 4 other people. Because of the math, it grows exponentially and more quickly," he says. "So, what seems like a fairly modest rate of infectivity can cause a virus to dominate very quickly."

2. Unvaccinated people are at risk.

In the U.S., there is a disproportionate number of unvaccinated people in Southern and Appalachian states including Alabama, Arkansas, Georgia, Mississippi, Missouri, and West Virginia, where vaccination rates are low. (In some of these states, the number of cases is on the rise even as some other states are lifting restrictions because their cases are going down). Kids and young people are a concern as well. "A recent study from the United Kingdom showed that children and adults under 50 were 2.5 times more likely to become infected with Delta," says Dr. Yildirim. And so far, no vaccine has been approved for children 5 to 12 in the U.S., although the U.S. and a number of other countries have either authorized vaccines for adolescents and young children or are considering them. "As older age groups get vaccinated, those who are younger and unvaccinated will be at higher risk of getting COVID-19 with any variant," says Dr. Yildirim. "But Delta seems to be impacting younger age groups more than previous variants."

3. Delta could lead to 'hyperlocal outbreaks.'

If Delta continues to move fast enough to accelerate the pandemic, Dr. Wilson says the biggest questions will be about the heightened transmissibility—how many people will get the Delta variant and how fast will it spread? The answers could depend, in part, on where you live—and how many people in your location are vaccinated, he says. "I call it 'patchwork vaccination,' where you have these pockets that are highly vaccinated that are adjacent to places that have 20% vaccination," Dr. Wilson says. "The problem is that this allows the virus to hop, skip, and jump from one poorly vaccinated area to another." In some cases, a low-vaccination town that is surrounded by high vaccination areas could end up with the virus contained within its borders, and the result could be "hyperlocal outbreaks," he says. "Then, the pandemic could look different than what we've seen before, where there are real hotspots around the country." Some experts say the U.S. is in a good position because of its relatively high vaccination rates—or that conquering Delta will take a race between vaccination rates and the variant. But if Delta keeps moving fast, multiplying infections in the U.S. could steepen an upward COVID-19 curve, Dr. Wilson says. So, instead of a three- or four-year pandemic that peters out once enough people are vaccinated, an uptick in cases would be compressed into a shorter period of time. "That sounds almost like a good thing," Dr. Wilson says. "It's not." If too many people are infected at once in a particular area, the local health care system will become overwhelmed, and more people will die, he says. While that might be less likely to happen in the U.S., it will be the case in other parts of the world, he adds. "That's something we have to worry about a lot."

4. There is still more to learn about Delta.

One important question is whether the Delta strain will make you sicker than the original virus. But many scientists say they don't know yet. Early information about the severity of Delta included a study from Scotland that showed the Delta variant was about twice as likely as Alpha to result in hospitalization in unvaccinated individuals, but other data has shown no significant difference. Another question focuses on how Delta affects the body. There have been reports of symptoms that are different than those associated with the original coronavirus strain, Dr. Yildirim says. "It seems like cough and loss of smell are less common. And headache, sore throat, runny nose, and fever are present based on the most recent surveys in the U.K., where more than 90% of the cases are due to the Delta strain," she says. Experts are starting to learn more about Delta and breakthrough cases. A Public Health England analysis (in a preprint that has not yet been peer-reviewed) showed at least two vaccines to be effective against Delta. The Pfizer-BioNTech vaccine was 88% effective against symptomatic disease and

96% effective against hospitalization from Delta in the studies, while Oxford-AstraZeneca (which is not an mRNA vaccine and is not yet available in the U.S.) was 60% effective against symptomatic disease and 93% effective against hospitalization. The studies tracked participants who were fully vaccinated with both recommended doses.

Moderna also reported on studies (not yet peer-reviewed) that showed its vaccine to be effective against Delta and several other mutations (researchers noted only a "modest reduction in neutralizing titers" against Delta when compared to its effectiveness against the original virus). "So, your risk is significantly lower than someone who has not been vaccinated and you are safer than you were before you got your vaccines," Dr. Yildirim says. But in August, the Biden administration said that, pending FDA clearance, it will offer all Americans who are fully vaccinated with the mRNA vaccines booster shots, and that could start as soon as late September. While there still needs to be an FDA determination that boosters will be safe and effective, officials recommended them as soon as September 20. They based their advisory on the spread of Delta and three recent studies from the CDC that suggested vaccine protection against infection is waning. In one of those studies, data from the state of New York showed vaccine effectiveness dropping from 91.7 to 79.8% against infection, although the vaccine continued to protect against hospitalization. Earlier this summer, Johnson & Johnson reported that its vaccine is effective against Delta, but another study suggested that its vaccine may be less effective against the variant, which prompted discussion over whether J&J recipients might also need a booster. In August, the company announced that new data showed a booster shot at six months had a rapid and robust nine-fold increase in spike-binding antibodies in volunteers compared to 28 days after their first dose. That data has not yet been peer-reviewed or published in a scientific journal. There are additional questions and concerns about Delta, including Delta Plus—a subvariant of Delta, that has been found in the U.S., the U.K., and other countries. "Delta Plus has one additional mutation to what the Delta variant has," says Dr. Yildirim. This mutation, called K417N, affects the spike protein that the virus needs to infect cells, and that is the main target for the mRNA and other vaccines, she says. "Delta Plus has been reported first in India, but the type of mutation was reported in variants such as Beta that emerged earlier. More data is needed to determine the actual rate of spread and impact of this new variant on disease burden and outcome," Dr. Yildirim adds.

5. Vaccination is the best protection against Delta.

The most important thing you can do to protect yourself from Delta is to get fully vaccinated, the doctors say. At this point, that means if you get a two-dose vaccine like Pfizer or Moderna, for example, you must get both shots and then wait the recommended two-week period for those shots to take full effect. Whether or not you are vaccinated, it's also important to follow CDC prevention guidelines that are available for vaccinated and unvaccinated people. "Like everything in life, this is an ongoing risk assessment," says Dr. Yildirim. "If it is sunny and you'll be outdoors, you put on sunscreen. If you are in a crowded gathering, potentially with unvaccinated people, you put your mask on and keep social distancing. If you are unvaccinated and eligible for the vaccine, the best thing you can do is to get vaccinated." Face masks can provide additional protection and the WHO has encouraged mask-wearing even among vaccinated people. The CDC updated its guidance in July to recommend that both vaccinated and unvaccinated individuals wear masks in public indoor settings in areas of high transmission to help prevent Delta's spread and to protect others, especially those who are immuno-compromised, unvaccinated, or at risk for severe disease. The agency is also recommending universal indoor masking for all teachers, staff, students, and visitors to K-12 schools. Of course, there are many people who cannot get the vaccine, because their doctor has advised them against it for health reasons or because personal logistics or difficulties have created roadblocks—or they may choose not to get it. Will the Delta variant be enough to encourage those who can get vaccinated to do so? No one knows for sure, but it's possible, says Dr.

Wilson, who encourages anyone who has questions about vaccination to talk to their family doctor. "When there are local outbreaks, vaccine rates go up," Dr. Wilson says. "We know that if someone you know gets really sick and goes to the hospital, it can change your risk calculus a little bit. That could start happening more. I'm hopeful we see vaccine rates go up."

Everything you need to know about the new coronavirus variant of interest, the world health organization (who) has added another coronavirus variant to its list to monitor. It's called the mu variant and has been designated a variant of interest (VOI). What this means is that the mu has genetic differences to the other known variants and is causing infections in multiple countries, so therefore might present a particular threat to public health. It's possible that mu's genetic changes might make it transmissible, allow it to cause more disease and render it a severe Immune response driven by vaccines or infections with previous variants. This in turn might leave it less susceptible to treatments. Note: the word might A VOC is not a variant of concern. (VOC) which is a variant that has been proven to acquire one of those characteristics, making it more dangerous and so more consequential. Mu is being monitored closely to see if it should be redesignated as a VOC. We have to hope not. In the meantime, Ida now a tropical storm as more than 1million Louisiana utility customers are left without power hurricane Ida made landfall in Louisiana on Sunday as a category 4 storm with winds of 150 miles an hour one of the strongest storms to hit the regions since hurricane Katrina Ida since has been downgraded to an tropical storm. And is expected to move farther inland over southeastern Louisiana and into the Southwestern Mississippi. After this morning the national hurricane center said. Maximum sustained winds have decreased to near 60 mph with higher gusts. As of early Monday, more than 1million Louisiana utility customers are without power, according to the power outage U.S. on Sunday evening. New Orleans said the entire city lost power after catastrophic transmission damage. In other parts of the world there are fires out of control and earthquakes floods, things out of our control there is sickness and diseases that are killing people every day. People are killing each other with guns, even children being killed. But there is a God that won't turn his back on us as we do him at times. It is hard to accept when your loved ones die but the Lord knows what's best for us. We just have to trust him. And look to him and his word. I believe this is the birth pains that the Bible talks about when there will be things happening and the Lord is bidding time so that more of his children will come to him and be saved. "Today is the day for salvation, before his coming. Come Lord Jesus Come!"

www.ingramcontent.com/pod-product-compliance
Lightning Source LLC
Chambersburg PA
CBHW071457070526
44578CB00001B/375